THE CARE AND
FEEDING OF YOUR
YOUNG EMPLOYEE

The Care and Feeding of Your Young Employee

A Manager's Guide to Millennials and Gen Z

Jamie Belinne

ISBN: 1974401413
ISBN 13: 9781974401413

CONTENTS

WHY DOES THIS BOOK MATTER TO YOU?

Gen Y (born in the 80s and 90s, and often called Millennials) is now the largest labor force, surpassing both Gen X and the Baby Boomers.[1] What's more, the Bureau of Labor Statistics is projecting that by 2020 the US will have the lowest labor participation rates in the workforce since the late 1970s,[2] so you'll need and want every good worker you can get. Most of your labor pool will be Gen Y.

Gen Z (born since the late 90s) is the largest segment of the entire population, so they are your future workforce and customer base. More importantly, they are already online

---

1 R. Fry, "This Year Millennials Will Overtake Baby Boomers," *Pew Research Center Fact Tank,* January 16, 2015, accessed September 2015, http://www. pewresearch.org/fact-tank/2015/01/16/this-year-millennials-will-overtake-baby-boomers/.

2 "Labor Force Projections to 2020: A More Slowly Growing Workforce," *Bureau of Labor Statistics Employment Outlook: 2010-2020,* February 21, 2012, accessed July 17, 2017, https://www.bls.gov/opub/mlr/2012/01/art3full.pdf.

and engaged, and they are starting to graduate college. If you are not learning about and connecting with them, your business is doomed.

Forbes places Gen Y buying power at approximately $200B,[3] and *Mashable* already puts the buying power of Gen Z at $44B, based on an average weekly allowance of close to $17—although that doesn't include the additional buying influence they have on their parents, which is considerable.[4]

Having spent nearly 30 years in human resources, recruiting, career counseling, and university teaching, I have helped thousands of employers hire and onboard young employees, and I've helped tens of thousands of college students find internships and post-graduate employment. During that time, I've seen some consistent challenges when it comes to the proper care and feeding of young employees, but the two youngest generations currently entering the workforce are presenting some unique challenges and opportunities for employers.

While most managers want me to "fix" their young employees, the truth is that the younger generations greatly outnumber the older generations. As such, it's in our best interest to learn and adapt so we can develop them to lead our companies into the future.

Consider the brands you've known and loved that tried to make younger generations adapt to their visions, rather

---

3 D. Schawbel, "10 New Findings About the Millennial Consumer," *Forbes*, January 20, 2015, accessed October 2016, http://www.forbes.com/sites/danschawbel/2015/01/20/10-new-findings-about-the-millennial-consumer/.

4 Sylvan Lane, "Beyond Millennials: How to Reach Generation Z," *Mashable*, August 20, 2014, accessed October 2015, http://mashable.com/2014/08/20/generation-z-marketing.

than evolving to meet their needs and expectations. How much Kodak film have you used lately? Do you still have Blockbuster tapes that need to be returned? These brands were pace-setters and pioneers when they started, but the marketplace evolved past them. You must be willing to let go of what has worked in the past and adapt to the new consumer environment, or your business will go extinct. Gen Y and Gen Z can help your business move into the future.

This book offers specific examples and tips to help you address the most common concerns and problems that I hear from employers with young employees. It's designed to help you understand the workplace challenges while taking full advantage of the many opportunities presented by the new generations of young employees. Because if you refuse to adapt to the needs and norms of the new generation, your business can be left behind.

The Care and Feeding of Your Young Employee

Young employees, regardless of when they were raised, generally need more care and attention than experienced staff members. An investment of time and attention in their early years will result in much more productive, engaged, loyal, and successful leaders in the future.

And let's be honest: When it comes to caring for employees, there's a lot more food being offered in the workplace than there was just a few decades ago. Recently, I participated in conducting a research survey of experienced academic leaders, and they consistently named "brings snacks" as a behavior exhibited by good leaders. Meanwhile, more companies are providing corporate cafeterias with free or discounted meals, often prepared by top chefs, as a way of recruiting, motivating, and retaining the best talent. So don't dismiss the importance of feeding—both literally and figuratively!

Over the years, I've worked with thousands of employers and young adults entering the workforce. I've found that there are five key workplace areas distinctly impacted by generational differences:

1. Expectations
2. Communication
3. Productivity
4. Motivation
5. Recruiting

Throughout the book, we will go over what each of these mean, how they impact your business, and the best practices for managing them effectively. I'll also share specific tips and examples for how to bring out the best in your Gen Y and Gen Z employees, as well as your entire team.

CHAPTER 1

5 GENERATIONS AT WORK— WHO ARE THEY?

E ach generation has been the new generation in the workforce at some point, and each one encountered challenges while adapting to the social and communication norms of the workplace. Most of this is a normal rite of passage. However, the challenge for Gen Y and Z is that so much has been said about them that people are often looking for behaviors to validate the stereotypes, rather than seeing them as individuals.

For example, here's a quick quiz for you. The statements below are all descriptions of people I have supervised in the past. Can you guess their generations?

A. Frequently on Facebook during work hours. Poor written communication skills. Needs explicit instructions.

B. Works to the point of illness, but comes into work anyway, despite risk of contagion and being told to reduce workload.

C. Doesn't work well in teams. Prefers to work with little oversight or involvement from others.

If you've been paying attention to popular reports on the generations, you probably guessed the following:

A. Gen Y
B. Baby Boomer
C. Generation X

Those would be great guesses based on generational stereotypes. However, here are the real answers for the specific, individual people I'm describing:

A. Baby Boomer
B. Generation X
C. Gen Y

I bring this up at the very beginning of our discussion on generational differences to make an important point: **Any explanation of generational behavior is based on trends and norms, and not on absolutes**. Generational context strongly influences the behavior of people in a generation, but their personal experiences and styles are ultimately what drive their individual decisions and actions. With that said, people within specific generations have many shared experiences driving their behaviors, so a look at generational differences is a great place to start when managing the diverse personalities within your organization.

Understanding the Generations

There are almost as many generations as there are books available on the subject. Below are just a few of my favorite names, none of which we'll be using in this book.

The Lost Generation	The Vocationals
Xennials	The Nonconformists
The Rioting Mobs	The Disengaged Generation
The Grinders	The Shopping Mall Generation
The Veterans	Selfie Generation
The Beat Generation	Generation O
The Uncommitted	The Draft Dodgers
The Disaffiliated	The Digital Generation
The Underachievers	The Greatest Generation
The Silent Generation	The ADD Generation
The Me Generation	The Young Radicals
The Sesame Street Generation	Generation Me

Again, I present these to point out that there are many ways to divide and describe people, and not all labels are positive or useful.

My experience is that specific date lines used to separate the generations are somewhat arbitrary and inconsistent, so we will use approximate date ranges. I've found that there are a few key "generational groups" defined by major world, cultural, and economic events. These are outlined below with the birth date ranges we will use for the purposes of this book.

Matures	Baby Boomers	Gen X	Gen Y/ Millennials	Gen Z
mid 1920s – mid 1940s	mid 1940s – mid 1960s	mid 1960s – late 1970s	late 1970s – late 1990s	late 1990s – ?

Each of these generations was profoundly impacted by the major events taking place while they were coming of age and developing their personalities. The context of their upbringing is the first glimpse through the window of who they are as a group.

Matures	Boomers	Gen X	Gen Y	Gen Z
World War II	Vietnam	Computers	Sept. 11	Mobile technology
Great Depression	Watergate	Video games	School shootings	Marriage equality
The New Deal	Women's Rights	Gulf War	Internet	Privacy issues
Rosie the Riveter	Civil Rights	Latchkey kids	Homeland security	Wi-Fi
	Television	MTV		

Thanks to improved healthcare, this is the first time since child labor laws were passed that we have five generations working together—although the bulk of the current workforce spans Boomers, Gen X, and Gen Y. I'll talk about each of these generations in the book, but we will focus on Gen Y and Gen Z—since they are becoming the vast majority of the workforce, and your ability to manage and motivate them will be critical to your success. But before we begin, let's do some overviews to get a better glimpse of how and why these groups are so different from each other.

Matures

The Matures are frequently called the "Silent" or "Traditional" generation, largely because they tended to be the least likely to rebel against authority or established tradition. This generation grew up during our nation's most difficult challenges, including the Great Depression, the Dust Bowl, World War II, and the Korean War.

Matures are generally described as:

Loyal
Patriotic
Resourceful
Respectful of authority
Responsible
Thrifty

The Matures grew up watching "Our Gang" (later known as "The Little Rascals") at the movie theater. If you've ever watched the show, then you know these children received almost no supervision or parenting whatsoever. They were expected to create their own entertainment, manage their own time and safety, and solve their own problems without any adult involvement. This mindset carried into the workforce.

The Fair Labor Standards Act wasn't passed until 1938, meaning many people in the Mature generation were in the workforce since childhood, which had a tremendous impact on their work ethic and attitudes. Another major factor was the Great Depression they experienced during their childhoods, which taught them to appreciate having a job.

At this stage, Matures are a very small percentage of the current workforce, although they had a tremendous impact on building our country and economy to the point where it is now. Because they are in the process of exiting the workforce, and because they have been in the workforce for so long, we will not spend time in this book describing how to manage them. However, I will point out that it is important to treat them with respect and honor to get their best work on the job. They are, in general, a very respectful and conservative generation that expects a certain amount of formality and traditionalism in the workplace.

Boomers
Baby Boomers were born during the period between the end of World War II and the mid-1960s when US birth rates were at an all-time high. The Baby Boomers grew up watching the Cleaver family on a black and white television on the hit show "Leave It to Beaver."

This was a traditional, intact family with a working father, homemaker mother, and two sons. It reflected the suburban migration of the time period. The Cleaver children were still given a tremendous amount of freedom to manage their own time and safety, and they attempted to solve their own problems, but involved adults as needed. The family is always well-dressed and well-behaved, the parents are always right, and the sons are always respectful. It basically reflects the ideal family the conservative Matures dreamed was possible with the country's newfound financial prosperity.

It's no surprise that the Boomers went through a period of rebellion against this perfectionism when they came of age during the Vietnam War and Watergate. Having experienced the disillusionment in discovering the imperfection of their parents' generation and the country's leadership, the Baby Boomers began to question the wisdom of their parents' loyal patriotism. However, they never let go of the ideal of the Cleaver family. As a result, Boomers are often described as:

Optimistic
Competitive
Individualistic
Questioning authority
Driven
Perfectionistic

Boomers' questioning of the status quo brought about tremendous social and cultural change. In their childhoods, they watched Walt Disney and American Bandstand, and drove up album sales for "rock and roll" music. As young adults, some Boomers became extremely politically active in Civil Rights, Women's Rights, and anti-war movements. Some even "dropped out" of the political world entirely and became "hippies."

It was only a short period between the Boomers' time as rebellious protesters or peaceful flower children and their transformation into competitive "Workaholics" (a term coined in 1971 by Wayne Oates). Because they are currently moving toward retirement, and because they are one of the most researched and documented generations already, I will not spend time discussing how to manage Baby Boomers in this book.

Gen X

With the availability of the birth control pill in the 1960s, birth rates rapidly declined, resulting in the smallest generation, Generation X. The Equal Pay Act and the Civil Rights Act were also passed in the 1960s, encouraging more women to enter and compete in the workplace. Divorce hit an all-time high during the childhoods of Gen X, and according to the US Census Bureau, more than 20% of Gen X was being raised in a single parent household.[5]

As the Boomers paved the way for future generations of women to have career success, Gen X became the "Latchkey Kid Generation." They were expected to be responsible from an early age, which made them more independent and involved in the family decision-making than in the past. As a result, when they entered the workplace, they expected to have a "seat at the table" sooner than the Boomers and Matures thought was reasonable or appropriate, based on their experiences.

As the Baby Boomers began the trends of executive mothers, increased divorce rates, and civil rights, the popular families in the media changed as well. More families headed

---

5   Ken Bryson and Lynne M. Casper, "Household and Family Characteristics: March 1997," *Census Bureau* P20-509 (April 1998), https://www.census.gov/prod/3/98pubs/p20-509.pdf.

by single mothers were featured in popular shows, such as "Alice" and "One Day at a Time." More blended and diverse families were also featured in "The Cosby Show," "The Brady Bunch," "Different Strokes," and "Sesame Street." By early adulthood, the disillusioned and cynical Generation X also became known as the "Slacker Generation," as illustrated in the 1991 movie "Slackers."

This became the first generation that saw non-traditional families and diversity as an expectation in our society. However, much like the Baby Boomers experienced disillusionment over their parents' key beliefs, Gen X also rebelled against what they perceived as their parents' focus on the corporate ladder and financial success.

As a result, Gen X entered the workplace focused on work-life balance and family values. They were major drivers in flex-time, mommy-track, job-sharing, 9-80 work weeks, and when the internet launched, they started telecommuting. Because all of these approaches continue to be useful and relevant tools, I will discuss them in detail in later chapters. Whereas previous generations often stayed at companies for a lifetime, Gen X saw companies eliminating pensions, offshoring jobs, and downsizing workforces. As a result, Gen X did not feel the same sense of corporate loyalty as previous generations, and they gained a reputation for leaving companies easily.

As a generation, Gen X is often described as:

Independent
Skeptical
Anti-traditional

Balanced
Flexible
Carpe Diem

This was the first generation for which the term "Boomerang Child" was used, since so many returned home at some point after college graduation due to job shortages and layoffs. Although, as they matured, this "Slacker Generation" was also the generation for whom the terms "Yuppie" (Young, Urban, Professional) and "DINK" (Dual Income, No Kids), were popularized. Because Gen X is already established in their careers, I will not discuss how to manage them in this book.

Gen Y

Also called Millennials, less than half of Gen Y was raised in "traditional" families.[6] They saw even more diverse and blended families on television than Gen X. "Full House," "Who's the Boss," "Charles in Charge," "Sister Sister," and even "Doogie Howser, MD" were all shows featuring non-traditional families where the children had as much say in family decisions as the adults.

Millennials were typically the product of aging Boomers who had postponed having children until their careers were established, or of Gen X parents who were determined to be more involved in their children's lives than the Boomers had been. In either situation, Gen Y had extremely doting and

---

6 G. Livingston, "Fewer Than Half of US Kids Today Live in a 'Traditional' Family," *Pew Research Center Fact Tank*, December 22, 2014, accessed October 2016, http://www.pewresearch.org/fact-tank/2014/12/22/less-than-half-of-u-s-kids-today-live-in-a-traditional-family/.

involved parents who involved them in most major family decisions and encouraged their personal development. The result was a generation often described as:

Confident
Collaborative
Achieving
Pressured
Overcommitted
Respectful of authority

According to the Centers for Disease Control and Prevention, the number of women 35-39 having their first child increased nearly seven-fold between 1970 and 1995.[7] So, in contrast to Gen X, a large number of Gen Y were born through fertility treatments to relatively older parents.[8] These were the dearly wanted and awaited miracle babies. Is it any wonder their parents became the "helicopter parents" who supervised their every move and cheered their every step?

Of course, the downside to being so loved and valued is the phenomenon that has some people calling Gen Y the "Soccer Trophy Generation." Much more than in previous generations, Millennials were rewarded for participation and collaboration rather than competition. This has result-ed in a generation that is much more team-oriented and

7   T.J. Mathews and B. Hamilton, "First Births to Older Women Continue to Rise," *NCHS Data Brief* 152 (May 2014), accessed July 5, 2017, https://www.cdc.gov/nchs/products/databriefs/db152.htm.

8   A. Chandra, C.E. Copen, and E.H. Stephen, "Infertility and Impaired Fecundity in the United States, 1982–2010: Data from the National Survey of Family Growth," *National Health Statistics Report* 67 (August 14, 2013), accessed July 5, 2017, https://www.cdc.gov/nchs/data/nhsr/nhsr067.pdf.

collaborative than previous generations. They are also more accustomed to frequent praise than previous generations.

In addition, helicopter parents raised the safest generation so far. Car seats, helmets, seat belt laws, and television rating systems were all marketed to protect Gen Y. All of this work seems to have had an impact, because the number of civil cases in our courts has decreased by half since the early 90s, possibly due to a greater focus on safety and prevention.[9]

This generation has always lived in a world where each person's health and safety was everyone's responsibility. That attitude goes into the workplace with Gen Y, where they are focused on companies with strong ethics and positive social values.

But before we stereotype Gen Y as never having rolled around without a seatbelt in the back of a station wagon on family trips, we should recognize some of the additional benefits of their attitudes toward safety. According to the Centers for Disease Control and Prevention, the number of teens who drink and drive has decreased by more than half since the early 1990s.[10] Teen smoking and alcohol use are also at their lowest rates since the 1970s.[11] And teen birth rates have decreased by more than 40% since the 1990s.[12]

9   "Civil Cases," *Bureau of Justice Statistics Office of Justice Programs*, accessed July 5, 2017, http://www.bjs.gov/index.cfm?ty=tp&tid=45.

10   "Teen Drinking and Driving," *CDC Vital Signs*, last modified October 2, 2012, accessed July 5, 2017, http://www.cdc.gov/vitalsigns/teendrinkinganddriving/.

11   R. Melina, "Teen Smoking, Drinking Hits Lowest Levels Since 1970s," *Live Science*, December 15, 2011, accessed October 2016, http://www.livescience.com/17497-teen-cigarette-alcohol.html.

12   S. Ventura, B. Hamilton, and T.J. Mathews, "National and State Patterns of Teen Births in the United States, 1940–2013," *National Vital Statistics Reports* 63, no. 4 (August 20, 2014), accessed July 5, 2017, https://www.cdc.gov/nchs/data/nvsr/nvsr63/nvsr63_04.pdf.

Some of these changes may be a result of increased supervision, but it's likely that much of the change is a result of Gen Y having more and better entertainment options. For earlier generations, there wasn't always much to do on the weekends—other than get into trouble with friends. Contrast that with Gen Y, who could have virtual play dates with any friend or relative anywhere in the world, at any time of day or night, through online gaming and social media. They never experienced the National Lampoon-style family vacation, because they had portable video players and gaming systems with headsets.

Basically, Gen Y was the first generation that never had to be bored. This is not a generation that tolerates boredom, inefficiency, bureaucracy, or monotony at work well. But neither do your customers, and Gen Y understands that.

Gen Z

Right around the turn of the millennium, Gen Z, sometimes called "iGen," was being born. Before they could speak, they were online. This is the first generation with few widespread, shared media experiences. They are more likely to get their entertainment from the internet than from television, and that media is more likely to be YouTube clips than a network series. They were also as likely to watch their parents' favorite reruns on TV Land or Netflix as they were to watch current programming. Regardless of that, the family TV show that best reflects Gen Z's world is the aptly named "Modern Family." It exemplifies this generation's assumption of diversity, and that all families now have non-traditional aspects.

Multi-racial and gay marriage is something they accept without question.

After the backlash from the helicopter parenting Gen Y received, Gen Z has been given more room to solve their own problems, which is easy for them with the internet. This is the generation that assumes for any problem, "there's an app for that." If the app doesn't exist, this generation will build it. Quickly. Like Gen X and Y, they also have a seat at the decision-making table with their parents. These things, in combination, have resulted in a generation described as:

Comfortable with diversity
Entrepreneurial
Multitasking
Independent
Interconnected
Resourceful

While they were too young to remember the tech bubble bursting, they experienced the financial meltdown of 2008. As a result, most of Gen Z grew up in families that experienced layoffs. This is likely one of the reasons that Gen Z is the most entrepreneurial generation ever. Nearly three out of four Gen Z students say they want to own their own business one day.[13]

Gen Z is the first "digitally native" generation, meaning they were using technology before they could even talk. They have known how to work a smart phone or tablet their entire lives,

---

13 D. Schawbel, "The High School Careers Study," *Millennial Branding,*
February 3, 2014, accessed October 1, 2016, http://millennialbranding.
com/2014/high-school-careers-study.

and they've never had to wonder about anything since Google was always readily available with the answers. And according to the Pew Research Center, nearly 75% of all teens have a smart phone.[11] In other words, even if a child doesn't have a smart phone, his friend has one, so the internet is always available without limits or supervision for Gen Z. This has resulted in a very independent and self-taught generation.

More importantly, since Gen Z has always operated in a world with social media and online collaboration tools, they are no longer constrained by geography, or even curfews. Classmates can meet on GroupMe for hours at night working on class projects, and friends from summer camp who live far away can FaceTime or Skype every night, as though they never left each other.

Why Can't They Be Like We Were?

The 1963 Musical "Bye Bye Birdie" had a delightful song with Mature parents lamenting their Boomer children, asking, "Why can't they be like we were—perfect in every way? What's the matter with kids today?" But before we judge the younger generations, recognize how easy it is for us to look back on the hazy, filtered memories of our own youths and tell ourselves how much better we were. But is that true? Let's look at what was said about the different generations in their youth, compared to what was said as they started to mature.

---

14 M. Anderson, "How Having Smartphones (or not) Shapes the Way Teens Communicate," *Pew Research Center Fact Tank*, August 20, 2015, accessed October 1, 2016, http://www.pewresearch.org/fact-tank/2015/08/20/how-having-smartphones-or-not-shapes-the-way-teens-communicate/.

Generation	Reputation as Young People	Upside Seen in Workplace Later
Boomers	Self-absorbed	Socially conscious
	Entitled	Philanthropic
	Spoiled	Driven
Gen X	Slackers	Innovators
	Entitled	Balanced lifestyles
	Materialistic	Independent
Gen Y	Me Generation	Technically competent
	Entitled	Team-oriented
	Needy	Open to feedback
Gen Z	Screen-addicted	Entrepreneurial
	Entitled	Independent
	Poor Communicators	Creative

It's worth noting that *every* generation has been accused of being "entitled" by the previous generation. It's safe to say entitlement is more a symptom of youth than a generational definition. Each new generation needs a certain amount of mentoring and coaching from previous generations to channel their enthusiasm into productive endeavors.

We Reap What We Sow: The Interconnectedness of Generations

Taking it all a step further and looking at the interconnectedness of each generation, notice how each generation's growth and achievements have shaped the strengths and challenges of the next. Ultimately, each generation evolves based on the growth and progress of the previous generation, and the new challenges created by that growth. Each generation demonstrates the evolution and change of our society over time.

Legacies of the Generation	Challenges of the Next Generation
Boomers: • Reliable birth control • Women's Rights, Civil Rights, Equal Pay Act	Gen X: • Lower birth rates • Working mothers • Latchkey kids
Gen X: • Flexible workplace • Work-life balance • No Child Left Behind • Technology revolution	Gen Y: • Helicopter parenting • Participation trophies • Standardized testing • Online gaming and socializing, easily bored
Gen Y: • Social media • Mobile technology • Cloud technology	Gen Z: • Phone addiction • Less in-person communication • Accustomed to immediate gratification

In truth, each generation has worried that the next would bring the world to ruin, when in fact they just brought change to the world. More often than not, the change that occurred evolved in response to the achievements of the previous generation. The challenge is managing the change and evolution so it is positive and productive. In the next few chapters, we'll discuss how to do this effectively in your workplace.

CHAPTER 2

EXPECTATIONS

Earlier this year, I received a call from a furious manager telling me his Gen Z intern had filed for unemployment benefits at the end of her internship. As a manager myself, I fully understood his frustration with having to manage the false claim. At the same time, I wasn't terribly shocked by the situation. The manager insisted, "How could she possibly not know that she wasn't eligible for unemployment compensation after an internship?" To which I replied, "Where would she have learned that? Gen Z grew up watching their family members apply for unemployment benefits during the Great Recession, but nobody explained to them how the process actually worked."

Our generational expectations are established by the world in which we grow up. Because the experiences of Gen Y and Gen Z are different from those of previous generations, their expectations are different as well. But the good news is their expectations can be managed.

How Generational Experiences Impact Expectations

Both Gen Y and Gen Z were raised in a time when students were told that if they met established standards, they would be promoted. This has always been their experience, so it's no wonder this assumption followed them into the workplace. In school, they were taught the most important thing they could do was to give right answers, quickly and often. Their assignments and tests were built around being able to answer questions and give facts related to the established standards for their grade levels.

Now I'm not criticizing standardized tests, since they do have a key role in education. But the preponderance of multiple choice tests has resulted in generations that are more equipped to answer questions than to ask them. From kindergarten through 12th grade, students are rewarded for raising their hands and giving the right answer to a question, or for bubbling in answer sheets with the right answers. There is less and less room in the modern education system for Socratic Method and critical essays. As a result, the younger generations are often accused of lacking critical thinking skills at work, since they can be quick to give recommendations and input without taking much time to reflect or ask questions.

However, while Gen Y and Z were not having as many critical conversations at school as previous generations, they were having more critical conversations at home. As a result, both Gen Y and Z are extremely comfortable talking to their elders as equals. They have always been included in their families' critical decisions, with their opinions having substantial impact on final outcomes. For that matter, the terms "Ma'am" and "Sir" are almost obsolete in our language. Where previous generations often considered these terms a sign of respect for elders, the later generations saw them as oppressive terms that created barriers to inclusion and openness.

As a result, these expectations and attitudes have been carried into the workplace. Neither Gen Y nor Gen Z have ever been relegated to the "children's table" nor sent outside so the adults could talk. When they are at work, they expect to be part of strategic decisions, and they expect to be invited to key discussions, even though they may have limited experience. This is also why they may be more interpersonally casual than previous generations, assuming they are on a first-name basis with everyone they meet, regardless of age, rank, or seniority. While this habit is sometimes infuriating to Matures and older Boomers—and it's an area where the younger generations can benefit politically from some gentle coaching—trends are showing that the workplace of the future will be flat, casual, and first-name. Ultimately, it's in your best interest to adapt to these trends if you want to recruit and retain the brightest young people.

Expectations of Authority and Oversight

Young employees are frequently criticized for making obvious mistakes or doing unthinkable things in the workplace. Bear in mind that they are inexperienced, not unintelligent, and with coaching they can do great things. The bigger challenge is the assumptions we make around their decision-making processes, because how they approach problems is different from previous generations.

Helping Gen Y Employees Make Good Decisions at Work

Being raised by helicopter parents, Gen Y was taught that their superiors were watching over them and that they would be taken care of as long as they did as they were asked. Remember those low rates of teen pregnancy and drinking? These were all young people who were not actively rebellious, but instead were more trusting of and connected to their elders. The good news is that they take feedback and direction in the workplace much better than the youth of previous generations.

Unfortunately or fortunately, depending on your management style, Gen Y has also been taught to get out of the way and let their elders take charge. Helicopter parents are serious business, and many Gen Y children grew up with the expectation of protection and close supervision. As adults, they've brought this mindset into the workplace. They expect their managers to be available for regular feedback and input, and they also expect their managers to be there to provide direct guidance for solving problems that may come along.

As a group, Gen Y is excellent about following directions. To the letter. In general, they don't resent and rebel against micromanaging as much as previous generations. However, they do get frustrated when they think their managers are withholding key information or not communicating clearly with them. Have no doubt that Gen Y is a generation of people pleasers, and they want to make their managers happy. They just need you to tell them exactly what they need to do to make you happy. They are very fast learners, so once you've clearly explained a task to them, they will try it for themselves, seek out your feedback, and quickly build their skills. They are perfectly capable of critical thinking once they have assurances that it is not only safe to take risks, but also that they will be recognized and rewarded for solving their own problems.

So how can you get the most out of Gen Y? Start by leveraging their different and fresh perspectives to find new approaches and ideas for old products and projects. It is imperative that you don't immediately dismiss new ideas when they bring them up, though, or you'll stunt future creativity and discussion. Actively encourage their ideas on products and projects. The more you have mentors available to encourage and help develop your young employees' ideas, the faster they'll grow. If they have an idea with holes in it, send them back to fill in the holes themselves. Teach them how to question their own assumptions. They'll learn from the process, and very quickly you'll have a top performer who brings you fully-formed, creative solutions to old problems.

This one, simple technique of sending them back to solve their own problems (rather than always telling them the answers or solving the problems for them) will give you a greater return on investment than any leadership development program you could buy.

Case Study: My Gen Y Wants Too Much of My Time
I have a relatively large team with many young employees, all of whom would like personal attention and mentoring from

me. To be honest, I didn't handle this well for quite some time. I would get so overwhelmed by the constant stream of e-mails, instant messages, and visits from people wanting my feedback and advice that I started getting abrupt and unresponsive, which quickly backfired in the form of young employees who were hesitant to approach me, even when they should have.

I already scheduled regular one-on-one meetings with my team leaders, and I didn't have the bandwidth for frequent one-on-ones with all of their direct reports as well, although they clearly needed to feel like I was accessible to them.

So I decided to set up annual one-on-ones with *every* member of the team. These meetings were not related to their performance reviews but instead were a chance for each of them to sit with me privately and tell me:

1. What's going well in their jobs?
2. What's not going well?
3. What are their career plans for the future?
4. How can I or the department better support them?

Even though it was only once a year, it opened a dialogue where they had my undivided attention, and it gave them the opportunity to talk honestly about themselves and their experiences in the office. It also helped me discover problem areas in the organization I might not have otherwise noticed, as well as growth areas for my teams that I hadn't considered. More importantly, by paying attention to their long-term goals, I was able to make sure our office could create opportunities to make them want to stay with us.

The result was a team that didn't expect my attention at a moment's notice, but they also felt safe enough to approach me when something important was going on. As a consequence, I continue to have high-performing teams with extremely low turnover.

This is just one example of how to keep your young employees focused and motivated. There are several ways you can approach this, and we will cover some of them in Chapter 5, "Motivation."

Case Study: Gen Y Quickly Responds to Feedback

A while back, I had a team of eight Gen Y students doing a project for a Fortune 100 company headquartered in Houston, TX. The team had never worked together before, and they received very little supervision or guidance from me on their work. The company had provided the students with an overview of the organization's business, the problem the team would be researching, and the various issues impacting the problem.

The team had weekly check-in meetings by e-mail with the corporate sponsor where they could ask questions and update the sponsor on their progress. At each meeting, they gave positive news about how well the team was working together and how much progress they were making. This went on for seven weeks, before the project sponsor asked to see a draft of their final presentation, which was due the following week. The students very proudly sent the sponsor a lovely Prezi presentation, complete with embedded videos and original graphics. To which the sponsor replied, "This is lovely, but you answered the wrong question. You investigated a peripheral issue rather than the main problem. I need you to do this over before your final presentation next week."

Not surprisingly, the team panicked. They asked me if I could ask the sponsor to accept their work, and I said no, because the sponsor was correct, and they should have gotten clarification sooner. The team scrambled for the next week and completely redid the entire project...correctly this time.

After their final presentation, both the sponsor and the team were thrilled with the deliverable. The students met with me afterwards and told me it had been the most challenging and educational experience they'd ever had. They all agreed the experience was both transformational and positive. They also learned how important it is to ask the right questions. In the end, it was not necessary to simplify the project. When given the resources and the support, Gen Y will work hard to make their managers happy, and they don't resent the lessons and feedback involved in the learning.

Helping Gen Z Employees Make Good Decisions at Work

Unlike Gen Y, Gen Z did not have quite as overly-involved parents. However, they still had very close relationships with their parents and also were very comfortable taking feedback and guidance from the older generation. Being digitally native, Gen Z was far more likely than Gen Y to find information on their own before asking for help. More to the point, Gen Z children were much more likely to be handed a tablet or smart phone as a "babysitter" while their parents were working at home, so they became adept at both entertaining and informing themselves online without their parents' assistance and oversight.

As well, because so many Gen Z children have cell phones, they were given much more freedom to explore than Gen Y—in part because their parents could monitor them remotely. Consequently, Gen Z is the most self-directed and entrepreneurial generation we have ever seen. Through mobile platforms, they can launch a business or build a brand with little or no up-front capital or business planning.

When it comes to learning, Gen Z was also more likely to be self-taught through online education and collaboration. In a 2015 post by Sparks & Honey, they gave the following statistics on Gen Z:

- 33% watch lessons online
- 32% collaborate with classmates online
- 52% use YouTube or social media for research assignments
- 72% of high schoolers want to start their own business one day[15]

Along those lines, while the home school movement started in the 1960s, it became legal in every state in the 1990s. Since then, it has slowly grown, picking up speed in the past few years—with more than 2 million home-schooled students

15 Sparks & Honey, "Meet Generation Z: Forget Everything You Learned About Millennials," *Slideshare*, June 17, 2014, accessed July 5, 2017, http://www.slideshare.net/sparksandhoney/generation-z-final-june-17.

estimated now.[16] Cyber Charters, which are virtual, online public schools, have rapidly taken hold—with more than 200,000 enrolled students in 2013.[17] Resources like TedX University, MOOCs (massive open online courses), and Khan Academy have made it possible for Gen Z to learn more, faster, and better in a way that meets their learning needs—with the best instructors in the country—all free of charge, right from the comfort of their mobile devices. As of this writing, Khan Academy's YouTube channel has more than 3 million subscribers. These days, many Gen Z students use their time at school to develop social skills and then self-teach in the evenings using online resources that put the best instructors in the world in the palm of their hands.

With technologies such as GroupMe, Skype, and FaceTime, students can continue discussions of class projects or personal projects with friends and like-minded individuals from around the world in real time. Whereas previous generations would struggle to meet friends before or after school for homework discussions, Gen Z has grown up knowing that if they couldn't find the answer online, they could work collaboratively to solve any problem.

As a result, they have never had to read a map or ask for directions, thanks to GPS and Google Maps. Likewise, they have never had an argument with a friend over song lyrics,

16 B. Ray, "Research Facts on Homeschooling," *National Home Education Research Institute*, March 23, 2016, accessed October 10, 2016, http://www.nheri.org/research/research-facts-on-homeschooling.html.

17 A. Molnar, G. Miron, L. Huerta, L. Cuban, B. Horvitz, C. Gulosino, J.K. Rice, and S.R. Shafer, "Virtual Schools in the U.S. 2013: Politics, Performance, Policy, and Research Evidence," *National Education Policy Center* (May 2, 2013), accessed July 5, 2017, http://nepc.colorado.edu/publication/virtual-schools-annual-2013.

because they can look up the answer to any question as soon as it occurs to them. And therein lies the challenge that is beginning to frustrate the older generations as Gen Z enters the workforce.

While Gen Z is used to immediate answers and immediate solutions, they are also used to solving problems independently. They have excellent critical thinking and independent problem-solving skills, which means Gen Z can sometimes charge ahead on a project without thinking to get permission or clearance. They may also be more comfortable sharing sensitive information with people outside of the company than you would be, since they were raised in a world of open source systems and crowdsourcing. Along those same lines, they are also less likely to cite sources or to see a problem with representing group work as individual work.

Case Study: My Gen Z Doesn't Respect the Hierarchy

A while back, I received a call from an organization seeking advice on how to handle a Gen Z student they had hired into their college internship program. The student had been complaining that he didn't have enough to do. Every time they gave him a project, he was able to complete it in almost no time using the resources and tools he knew were available. When more challenging projects weren't forthcoming, he took it upon himself to come up with more work.

Unbeknownst to his supervisor, the student reached out to some clients to ask about services they would like to see offered. From this, he got the idea that their organization should offer financial training to clients. The student took it a step further by calling a company in New York to negotiate a third-party training contract, and then he worked with local hotels to set up training dates. In the end, the student couldn't understand why his manager was so angry when he presented him with the contracts to sign for the program. It never occurred to the student that he shouldn't reach out to clients without approval and that he shouldn't negotiate programs or set up events without involving a supervisor on the front end.

Going forward, the organization has set much clearer expectations with new interns, pointing out that any outreach on behalf of the organization requires prior approval, as do any new ideas, programs, or market research.

As you can see from this example, Gen Z is very different from Gen Y, and many companies aren't ready. Just as some companies have finished developing detailed training programs and processes to ensure the success of Gen Y, Gen Z comes along and assumes these are mere guidelines. As a group, Gen Z is much more likely to rush to closure on a project than previous generations, so proofreading, citations, and fact-checking skills may still need some coaching. However, like Gen Y, they still want their managers' approval, they still want to work collaboratively, and they still expect to be included in key decisions and discussions.

While not as many managers have dealt with Gen Z yet, be prepared for a group that is much less likely to seek out your input—although they still want your approval and recognition. Rather than setting clear expectations for taking initiative, as many have needed to do with Gen Y, you will more likely need to set clear expectations for limits of authority and decision-making with Gen Z. With that said, don't make the limits so restrictive that you stunt their creativity. This generation more than any before is likely to quit working for you to start their own business if they think their ideas and input aren't valued.

Case Study: Gen Z Sees the Problem and Solves It

Recently, there was a new high school being built in Pearland, Texas, and the middle school students who were scheduled to be the first Freshman class began discussing the kinds of classes they'd like to see. A group of friends started talking about how nice it would be to have a health professions track in the new school. One of the students asked a teacher what it would take to start something like this, and the teacher said it was up to the school board.

That night the students connected in GroupMe and decided they should talk to the school board. With the help of a teacher, the students were placed on the agenda for the next meeting. Meanwhile, the students started meeting online at night to plan their strategy. They divided the work, so some students researched existing health professions tracks in high schools. Others researched the job market projections for health professions. One gathered information on potential corporate partners in the area for the program. Lastly, they reached out to adults in their networks to ask for guidance on fundraising, speech writing, and presentations.

In the end, the students created a petition and launched it through social media to garner several hundred signatures from adult voters in the area. They used Google Docs to collaborate on their speeches and presentation, and they rehearsed their presentation online from home at night using Skype and GroupMe. This small group of 13-year-olds presented to the school board and directly impacted the curriculum of the school they would be attending without ever meeting or practicing in person prior to their presentation— and with almost no adult assistance or oversight. The moral of the story is that non-disclosure discussions and agreements may be more necessary with your Gen Z employees than with previous generations, because collaboration is so second nature to them.

As you can see, Gen Z are unstoppable to a fault when they see a larger purpose in their work. However, if you can channel their enthusiasm, they are tremendously productive. They simply need guidance and oversight, like any young, inexperienced worker.

Young Employees Who Want Promotions Without "Paying Their Dues"

The complaint that young employees want too much too soon has been made about young employees long before Gen Y or Gen Z hit the workplace. However, the challenge is still very real for managers, and it shows up differently for different generations.

The experience may look something like this:

<u>Gen X Manager says</u>: "Please join me in congratulating Susan on her promotion to Project Lead for the Southern Region."

<u>What Gen Y thinks</u>: *How did she get that promotion? I was hired six months before she was. That's not fair. I've never gotten into trouble and I've done everything they asked me to do. I think the manager just hates me. I should probably get a new job, because they're never going to promote me here.*

<u>What Gen Z thinks</u>: *What does "Project Lead for the Southern Region" mean? Sounds made up. It's so unfair that the people who do the least actual work are the ones getting paid the most. Last time I asked Susan about "Agile," she thought I was talking about Cirque du Soleil. I'll just get my work done and stay out of her way.*

Gen Y and Promotion Expectations

Gen Y was raised with the idea that if you do as you're told, you'll be rewarded. This belief was reinforced through standardized tests and participation trophies over many years. In the workplace, this translates into the notion that if you meet your manager's expectations, you should be promoted. As a result, this can lead to misunderstandings with Gen X and Boomer managers who were taught that only those who *exceed* expectations will get promoted. To correct this misunderstanding, Gen X and Boomer managers do NOT need to lower their expectations as Gen Y is perfectly capable of achieving high standards. You just need to be clear on what those standards actually are.

This is why many successful companies have eliminated the traditional annual review with numerical performance rating systems. If you think about it, if someone is consistently exceeding the expectations for the role, then maybe you weren't expecting enough in the first place! A more effective technique is to sit down with your Gen Y employee and be very clear on the outcomes and timelines you expect from them. Scheduling regular feedback discussions based on projects or goals with shorter time horizons, rather than annual performance meetings, yields a much more focused, effective, and productive employee.

Set your expectations "achievably high" so it is a stretch goal without being an impossible goal. Then let them go!

Gen Z and Promotion Expectations

Gen Z has a different perspective than Gen Y in that their experience was defined during economic downturns, ethical crises, and low employment rates for new college grads. Thus, they have less trust for the older generations and more faith in their own abilities. They've operated autonomously to solve problems throughout their lives, so the idea of a seemingly arbitrary hierarchy for decision-making may not fit their worldview easily.

However, Gen Z does understand financial reward systems, and the idea that financial rewards are tied to performance outcomes makes sense to them. Gen Z works best when given performance outcomes that are achievably high, with limited oversight of the process and short time horizons. Unlike Gen Y, Gen Z will need clearly defined limits of scope and authority when they are given work or placed into a hierarchy. This is another group that responds well to clear and honest expectations, with the addition of clear and honest limits.

So how can Gen X and Boomer managers deal with this? It is important for young employees to have the opportunity for regular one-on-one discussions, ideally with their managers, but at least with experienced mentors, so these things can be discussed before they become a problem.

In the best companies, young employees are encouraged to come up with a career plan outlining where they would like their careers to go in the company. Once the manager is aware of the goal, he or she works with the employee to develop a list of skills and experiences that will help the employee work toward that goal. Ideally, the employee will be encouraged to do an informational meeting with someone already in the desired role. This gives them a chance to learn what it takes to succeed in that job and what's needed to ultimately land it. Then it is the employee's job to report back to the manager/mentor at regular intervals in their one-on-one meetings—with updates on their professional accomplishments, progress, and obstacles—so the development plan can be updated.

Manage expectations early about reasonable timelines for growth so young employees will know up front if it typically takes one year or five to reach the next level in their careers. The more clear and transparent you are from the start, and the more you engage them in the process, the less misunderstanding there will be in the long run.

Does Everyone Expect a Participation Trophy?

Much has been said about the hyper-involvement of Gen Y and Gen Z in extracurricular activities. Many exhausted parents complain about spending their lives attending soccer practice, band recitals, dance competitions, gymnastics meets, intramural team competitions, and an assortment of other after-school activities. This is a no-win area for the younger generations. People criticize them for having too much "screen time," with some estimates as high as 20 hours/week. At the same time, the younger generations are also criticized for having too many activities outside of school. And on top of that, they are criticized for spending too much time on homework while still falling behind academically. What's going on here?

First, there are far more opportunities for involvement than there were for previous generations. The younger generations, who are gifted multitaskers, take full advantage of them all. Secondly, involved parents want to make sure their children have every opportunity to gain the experiences and skills necessary to succeed. Those aren't well-defined, so they allow their children to try a wide variety of activities while deciding where to focus.

Gen Y was criticized for being a generation where "everyone gets a trophy." Much like the backlash against helicopter parents resulted in more independence for Gen Z, the "soccer trophy" criticisms also resulted in a more competitive environment for them. Consequently, there is a noticeable decline in non-competitive soccer leagues, which are being replaced by highly competitive soccer leagues with tournaments around the globe, even at a very young age. This is true for almost all sports. In addition, dance classes are no longer about annual dance recitals, but instead about frequent dance competitions. Even cheerleading is now a competitive sport. (Who cheers for the cheerleaders?) While Gen

Z is highly collaborative, they also watched the struggles their older siblings had in the college application and job search processes, and they know they must compete to survive.

Let's look at that a little more closely. Gen Y is the most educated generation ever. This is great, except it means competition is extremely fierce for the best jobs, even at the professional levels, because there are so many college-educated people in the workforce now. Granted, you're much better off with a college degree than without one, since the US Census says college graduates, on average, earn about $1M more in their lifetimes than high school graduates.[18] At the same time, it's estimated that 44% of college graduates are underemployed at graduation.[19] So you must be able to compete to get the best jobs.

But competition isn't new for Gen Y. They were woefully unprepared for the realities of college admissions when their relatively large generation started to apply to their parents' alma maters. As the population has increased, top colleges have become increasingly selective to maintain enrollment rates. And while new universities, community colleges, and online universities have sprung up to meet student demand, the admissions rates for the more established universities have been steadily shrinking.

---

18 "The Big Payoff: Educational Attainment and Synthetic Estimates of Work-Life Earnings," *US Census* P23-210 (July 2002), accessed July 5, 2017, https://www.census.gov/prod/2002pubs/p23-210.pdf.

19 J. Abel, R. Deitz, and Y. Su, "Are Recent College Graduates Finding Good Jobs?" *Federal Reserve Bank of New York Current Issues in Economics and Finance* 20, no. 1 (2014), https://www.newyorkfed.org/medialibrary/media/research/current_issues/ci20-1.pdf.

For instance, let's take a look at the difference for a Boomer, a Gen X, a Gen Y, and a Gen Z who applied to Harvard.

Admit Year	Admission Rate
1965	20%
1993	18%
2006	9.7%
2015	5.3%

Sources: Thompson 2015, Lee 1993

You may be thinking, "Yes, but that's Harvard. The state schools are always a great option for higher education." According to their admissions websites in 2015, The University of Texas at Austin only admitted 40% of applicants. The University of Michigan only accepted 32%, and UC-Berkeley accepted 17%. Many older generations had the benefit of open enrollment in state universities if they graduated from a state high school. Those days are largely over.

As a result, students start competing in elementary school so they can take the classes in middle school that will allow them high school credit. Then once they reach middle school, they compete for limited seats in the Advanced Placement classes in high school and contend for spots on the sports teams and competition bands at their future high schools. Once in high school, they are vying for class rank and opportunities to demonstrate both leadership and community service so they can compete to get into college. By the time college arrives, they must again be top-ranked academically while holding leadership roles and internships in order to land the best jobs. It's a much more competitive world than anything the previous generations ever experienced. Frankly, Gen Y was not prepared for this level of competition, and Gen Z learned from watching them.

Gen Z is the multitasking generation that will do it all, all at once, because they have to.

For Gen Y, team recognition programs are useful in meeting their expectations for acknowledgment. Specific details on ways to do this without spending undue amounts of time and money are covered in Chapter 5, "Motivation." While Gen Z also responds well to team recognition, as a generation, they are more likely to compete for individual recognition and are less interested in recognition for involvement in the team. With that said, well-earned, specific praise and recognition is appreciated by all generations.

Best Practices for Managing Expectations

1. Gen Y prefers specific instructions and deadlines where it is clear how they can meet the manager's expectations. This means managers should be both specific and honest not only with what they expect,

but also if they would be happier if the employee exceeded the stated goal.

2. Gen Z prefers more autonomy when working, so it is important to be clear not only on expectations, but also on the limits of their authority and when/where they should request approvals.

3. Young employees should have regular one-one-one meetings with their managers and, if possible, with experienced mentors in the company to ensure they not only have reasonable expectations, but also that they understand how to progress on their goals.

4. Employees should develop and share career goals with their managers and mentors, and then managers should develop reasonable timelines and outline the steps required to move toward these goals with the employee.

5. Acknowledge both team involvement on projects as well as individual performance.

CHAPTER 3

COMMUNICATION STYLES

I had a top investment bank complain to me that one of their star recruits was seriously underperforming in his internship. While the intern was doing the work requested, he spent the bulk of his time on social media rather than learning new skills or networking with co-workers. When I talked to the intern, it had simply never occurred to him that, as an intern, he would be expected to do more than the work requested of him. He was very interested in a full-time offer, so I encouraged him to put away his phone, ask his manager about upcoming projects in the company, and then find ways to add extra value to those projects. Using this approach, he then took the initiative to work overnight doing research on the impending project so he could present his preliminary findings and analysis to his manager the morning they were scheduled to begin research, even though it wasn't a requested task. Yes, he got the full-time offer at the end of the internship. He was a smart and driven student. He just needed someone to clearly explain what was actually expected.

Another challenge for many young employees is assertive communication. These generations were shaped through anti-bullying campaigns and political correctness, which were extremely useful in many ways, but were sometimes taught at the expense of healthy, assertive communication skills. As a result, you get situations like the one I'm about to share.

Not long ago, I had a student who accepted an internship at the headquarters of a large global retailer. A week after she started her internship, her employer called me to say that she'd disappeared. Frightened for her safety, I called the student and her family members until she called me back. It turns out she had decided to quit the internship, but she wasn't comfortable telling her manager, so she just left—assuming he would figure out that she'd quit. When I asked why she quit, she said the work was harder than she'd expected, and she decided it was better to quit than to fail (which was another issue we dealt with). I also asked why she didn't ask her manager for training and assistance, since it was an internship, and she said she didn't want to bother him!

Needless to say, we had a coaching moment. But the lack of assertive communication skills is another challenge with the younger generations, where online communication has served as a shield between them and direct, difficult conversations.

My Young Employee Can't Communicate

Before I go into the theories about cause, I will state up front that we are seeing a decline in writing skills nationally. I want to balance this with the findings of a recent research study by The University of Michigan, which showed that people who are easily irritated by spelling and grammar issues tend to have personality assessment scores that would correlate with being difficult people to work with.[20] (I intentionally ended that sentence with a preposition, so you could see if it bothered you.) In general, writing skills are on the decline, but the tradeoff may be a more collaborative and creative workplace, and the decline in writing skills is not entirely a generational issue.

With a nearly 40% increase in the number of college degrees conferred between 2001 and 2012, Gen Y has the highest level of educational attainment of any previous generation.[21] There was a surge in college-preparatory programs available to Gen Y during their childhoods, and these programs paid off in terms of college enrollment and graduation rates. Also, in 2001, the No Child Left Behind Act was passed, launching a new era of standards-based education. The Educational Testing Service became a key resource for assessing the performance of our students compared to students around the world. Below is an excerpt from their 2015 report:

"[T]hese young adults on average demonstrate relatively weak skills in literacy, numeracy, and problem solving

---

20   Julie Boland and Robin Queen, "If You're House Is Still Available, Send Me an Email: Personality Influences Reactions to Written Errors in Email Messages," *PLOS ONE* (March 9, 2016), accessed July 5, 2017, http://journals.plos.org/plosone/article?id=10.1371/journal.pone.0149885.

21   Thomas D. Snyder, Cristobal de Brey, and Sally A. Dillow, "Digest of Education Statistics 2015, 51st Edition," *Institute of Education Sciences National Center for Education Statistics* (December 2016), https://nces.ed.gov/pubs2016/2016014.pdf.

in technology-rich environments compared to their international peers. These findings hold true when looking at Millennials overall, our best performing and most educated, those who are native born, and those from the highest socioeconomic background. Equally troubling is that these findings represent a decrease in literacy and numeracy skills for U.S. adults when compared with results from previous adult surveys.

- *In literacy, U.S. Millennials scored lower than 15 of the 22 participating countries. Only Gen Y in Spain and Italy had lower scores.*
- *In numeracy, U.S. Millennials ranked last, along with Italy and Spain.*
- *In PS-TRE [Problem Solving in a Technology-Rich Environment], U.S. Gen Y also ranked last, along with the Slovak Republic, Ireland, and Poland.*
- *The youngest segment of the U.S. Gen Y cohort (16- to 24-year-olds), who could be in the labor force for the next 50 years, ranked last in numeracy along with Italy and among the bottom countries in PS-TRE. In literacy, they scored higher than their peers in Italy and Spain."[22]*

One of my roles as a university instructor for the past decade has been to administer thousands of writing assessments to college students. Every student I teach has passed at least two college-level English classes before I see them. More than 60% of these students took English through community colleges

22   R. Coley, M. Goodman, and A. Sands, "America's Skills Challenge: Millennials and the Future," *Educational Testing Service*, February 17, 2015, accessed July 5, 2017, https://www.ets.org/s/research/29836/.

or online programs—and then transferred the credits to the university in an effort to reduce their total educational costs—so I have limited information on their curricula. My writing assessment requires them to write a business memo in response to a given scenario. I have found that nearly 5% of students who have already passed six hours of college-level English cannot write what most managers would consider a "good" memo, and they therefore require additional training in writing.

In addition, because so many students have grown up casually communicating through text and instant messaging, the basic skills of being clear, persuasive, and accurate in writing have not been actively practiced. I do not blame the students entirely for this situation. As the ratio of students to teachers has grown, students are doing less writing in school. Teachers do not always have the resources to commit the additional time required to grade large numbers of research papers, and they are evaluated on preparing their students for standardized tests.

When Generation X entered the workforce, companies complained to schools that young people were not being trained to work in teams or make presentations. School systems worked hard to remedy this situation, and the result is that students are now doing most of their school work in groups and then presenting their final deliverables as a team PowerPoint or Prezi rather than as individually written research papers. Therefore, the new generations are extremely talented using more visual media than previous generations.

Generations Y and Z may not have been trained with the same emphasis on spelling and grammar as previous generations, but they are often gifted at creating attractive and compelling presentations in ways previous generations are not. With most software already having spell check and grammar check, the ability to make an interesting presentation is becoming more critical than the ability to spell. Spell check and grammar check are not perfect, but with ongoing improvements in artificial intelligence, they are becoming better every day. While Gen Y and Gen Z may not be ideal to meet the communication needs of older generations, they are often more skilled for the future demands of communication with their own generations, which we've already established are your growing customer base.

Ultimately, their communication skills are simply evolving to be better suited to the new media becoming prevalent.

Leverage these skills. Use Gen Y to develop attractive videos and Prezi presentations. Most people would rather read an infographic than a report, anyway, and Gen Y knows how to do this better than you do. Let them work and present in teams. Tap into their experiences to guide your social media presence and campaigns. And as Gen Z enters your workforce, leverage their natural abilities and experience with social media and video to prepare compelling and engaging presentations for your next generation of customers. This is a group that learned more from YouTube than they did in the classroom, so they know how to design a video that is compelling and engaging for your customers.

Attention to detail is still important. At the same time, your new customers will focus more on attractive and interactive communication than spelling and grammar. With an average attention span of eight seconds for adults in North

America (which is one second shorter than a goldfish's[23]), nobody is reading your documents, anyway.

My Young Employee Speaks Emoji

With the evolution of communication and the reduction of attention spans, people don't read much anymore. That's not a generational statement. It's a cultural statement. In 2014, Pew Research found that 23% of *all* adults had not read a book in the past year, compared to only 8% in 1978 when Gallup conducted the same research.[24] All of the information people need or want can be found on the internet in bite-sized pieces. Entertainment is largely in the form of video, podcast, or online gaming. Even as I write my own books, I recognize that most people will skim the graphs and lists more than they will read—which is why I'm such a heavy user of graphs and lists.

The shift in communication styles we see in the younger generations is a result of a larger cultural shift, and has little or nothing to do with their ability to think or communicate. Social media has become the new water cooler, and the communication style of the younger generations has just evolved to adapt to the changing environment in which they live.

Gen Y and Gen Z communicate succinctly and visually. In our own way, we have almost come full circle back to the

---

23   Kevin McSpadden, "You Now Have a Shorter Attention Span Than a Goldfish," *Time*, May 14, 2015, accessed July 5, 2017, http://time.com/3858309/attention-spans-goldfish/.

24   J. Weissmann, "The Decline of the American Book Lover," *The Atlantic*, January 21, 2014, accessed July 5, 2017, http://www.theatlantic.com/business/archive/2014/01/the-decline-of-the-american-book-lover/283222/.

pictograms of Mesopotamia and Ancient Egypt. Do you think I'm wrong? Have you ever looked at the texts of a Gen Y or Gen Z person? There are frequently more emojis than words. For example, the following is from the "Emojipedia" for Snapchat regarding emojis that appear next to Snapchat contact names:

Face With Sunglasses — *One of your best friends is one of their best friends. You send a lot of snaps to someone they also send a lot of snaps to.*

Grimacing Face — *Your #1 best friend is their #1 best friend. You send the most snaps to the same person that they do. Awkward.*

Smirking Face — *You are one of their best friends…but they are not a best friend of yours. You don't send them many snaps, but they send you a lot.*

Gold Star — _Someone has replayed this person's snaps in the past 24 hours. They must have something interesting to show._

Fire – _You are on a Snapstreak! You have snapped this person every day, and they have snapped you back. Increases with number of consecutive days._

Hundred — _100 Day Snapstreak. The 100 emoji appears next to the fire when you snap back and forth with someone for one hundred days in a row._

Source: Emojipedia

I provide this to make an important point. There are hundreds of emojis, and Gen Z knows what they all mean. How long would it take you to learn just the list above? Probably not long, but you're also probably not going to bother. And why is that? Because if you're Gen X or older, you're most likely not using Snapchat, so the emojis aren't important to your life and success. But Snapchat has more than 100 million daily users, so understanding that social language is of critical importance to younger generations in developing their networks, their personal brands, and in some cases, their businesses. More and more businesses are finding tremendous marketing success through Snapchat daily, while older generations can't even speak the "language" of the communication channel.

By the way, for those of you in the Gen X and older categories, I should warn you that the consensus among my Gen Z students is that "Facebook is for old people." The usage demographics support this statement. According to GlobalWebIndex, approximately 15% of 16-to 24-year-olds were using Facebook in 2014, compared to 40% using Instagram.[25] With the increasing popularity of smart phones, making it easy to instantly load photographs online, the younger generation realized they preferred loading pictures to loading text, and Instagram took over. Communication is becoming visual rather than textual.

Let's go back to Snapchat for a minute. It is rapidly becoming the most popular form of communication and news gathering for the younger generations. Why is that? Taking a step backwards, one of the dangerous things that started to evolve as young people had greater access to social networks was a loss of privacy. For older generations going to college, if you opened the camera and exposed the film, then nobody could prove the night ever happened. But when Gen Y got to college, those days were over. Every mistake, misstep, or bad idea was captured, posted, and circulated before you could say, "I'm sorry." Largely in reaction to this, Snapchat was born.

Posts to Snapchat can be set to exist for 10 seconds to 24 hours, and the audience can also be controlled by the poster. It's brought a small amount of privacy and control back to the lives of young people, even when they are surrounded by smart phones with cameras. As one Gen Z person told me about Snapchat, "I like it because you can post karaoke videos during a party, but they're gone the next morning." Whisper offers a visually engaging platform to share private confessions in a public forum with complete anonymity.

25 J. Mander, "Facebook Slips as Instagram Rises," *GlobalWebIndex*, February 9, 2015, accessed July 5, 2017, http://www.globalwebindex.net/blog/facebook-slips-as-instagram-rises.

The list of apps is endless and always changing. Imagine the possibilities!

Here's the real question, though: Do you know how to optimize these communication channels and styles, or do you try to simply make the same old messages fit into the new formats? Are you posting flyers about your recruiting events, or posting to Snapchat? These young people live on these platforms, so if you're not actively engaged in their world, your business isn't part of their world, either.

Eastman Kodak invented the core technology used in digital cameras, but it didn't embrace digital and was slow to truly accept that traditional photography was dying. As a result, one of the historically strongest technology companies in the US filed for bankruptcy protection in 2012, because it took too long to accept change.[26] Kodak refused to accept that the world was changing radically and quickly, and they rested on more than a century of success to support their decisions. They refused to evolve, because they didn't like what evolution looked and felt like.

The same is true when it comes to the evolution of communication skills. The companies who leverage the gifts of the younger generations' visual and succinct communication skills will be the ones to connect with this tremendous segment of the consumer market.

To be clear, written communication skills are still critical. That's why I do writing assessments in my university classes. But it's likely that an acceptable and appropriate business memo in the future will look very different from what we

---

26 M. Hiltzik, "Kodak's Long Fade to Black," *Los Angeles Times*, December 4, 2011, accessed July 5, 2017, http://articles.latimes.com/2011/dec/04/business/la-fi-hiltzik-20111204.

consider an acceptable and appropriate business memo right now.

Our language is both simplifying and evolving. The slang of yesterday is the vernacular of today. While many of us were terrified that LOL and NBD (Laugh Out Loud and No Big Deal) would take over our language, the proliferation of the smart phone and autofill have brought us back to full words again. A few years ago, I ended a lecture on decision-making with a slide that said, "YOLO," to which one of my students replied, "I guess if the professors are using it, the word must be old now!" (YOLO=You Only Live Once.)

If you want to have an engaged workforce and an engaged customer base, your business is going to have to evolve with them.

Case Study: Taco Bell and Snapchat

Taco Bell was an early adopter of Snapchat, and with more than 200,000 friends, it boasts a 90% view rate for its posts.[27] Unlike traditional advertising, Snapchat has allowed the fast food giant to directly target Gen Y and Gen Z through pictures, videos, and time-sensitive offers. They launched the comeback of their "Beefy Crunch Burrito" through a picture on Snapchat. They do relevant, current, and entertaining videos and photo montages on the site. One Valentine's Day,

---

27 G. Sloane, "Snapchat's 'Crazy Engaged' Users Can't Resist a Message From Taco Bell," *Adweek*, August 22, 2014, accessed July 5, 2017, http://www.adweek.com/news/technology/snapchats-crazy-engaged-users-cant-resist-message-taco-bell-159677.

they created a Valentine's card that Snapchat users could screenshot, personalize, and then re-post to a friend.[28]

Recognizing that Gen Y tends to impulsively snack around the clock, rather than eating just three scheduled meals a day, Taco Bell took advantage of Snapchat to reach them 24 hours a day, engaging them with interesting content to catch them whenever they're hungry. One of their Snapchat videos during the MTV Movie Awards incited a social media frenzy while announcing the arrival of the Spicy Chicken Cool Ranch Doritos Locos Tacos.[29] Traditional channels can't provide that kind of buzz in the Gen Y and Gen Z target markets.

Helping Your Young Employee to Write and Speak Better

This is achievable, but it will take intervention to train them on how you want them to communicate. To do this, managers must *consistently* model good communication standards. While the manager may clearly understand when informal communication is acceptable and when more formal communication is needed, the young employee will only see that informal communication is accepted in the organization. Also, managers must be comfortable giving specific, constructive, and direct feedback to young employees about their written

28   T. Dua, "Inside Taco Bell's Snapchat Strategy," *Digiday*, August 13, 2015, accessed July 5, 2017, http://digiday.com/brands/inside-taco-bells-snapchat-strategy/.

29   E. Epstein, "Why Taco Bell Went Loco for Snapchat and Millennials," *Mashable*, May 29, 2014, accessed July 5, 2017, http://mashable.com/2014/05/29/taco-bell-marketing-strategy/#RGGLD1s9uiqj.

and verbal communication. They are very open to feedback when it is given in a constructive and achievable way.

For example, I have had to catch employees one-on-one after an internal presentation to say, "Did you know that you sometimes say 'aks' instead of 'ask'?" or "I'm not sure if you realize how many times you say 'OK?' when you present, but it makes you seem uncertain, which can make your listeners doubt your message." I have hired speaking coaches to work with young employees when necessary, and I've referred others to Toastmasters, especially their Young Professionals groups.

Written communication can be more difficult to fix. However, they can learn quickly if you set clear expectations, model good communication, and give frequent feedback. For instance, it may be necessary to set standards for e-mail conversations that include some of the following rules:

1. All e-mails should start with a salutation.
2. All e-mails must be run through spell check and grammar check before sending. (And they must be corrected before they are sent.)
3. E-mails dealing with sensitive or emotional issues should be reviewed by a manager or co-worker before they are sent.
4. All employees will have a standard signature line containing a closing line, their name, title, company name, phone number, e-mail, and web address.

While these things may seem like common sense, they are learned behaviors, and they can be easily taught. You can extend these policies to cover all published materials, since not all software automatically runs spell check or grammar check. If you have the resources, designating a manager to review and give coaching on a young employee's materials before they are published is the best practice until you are confident in the employee's abilities.

How to Give Verbal Direction By Generation

Communication needs will vary by individual, but there are some trends we can see across generations that impact how they prefer to receive instruction as well as how they respond to different kinds of instructions.

Both Boomers and Generation X were defined in part by their rebellions against the attitudes and cultural norms of their parents' generations. As a result, when they entered the workforce, they worked best with limited oversight and supervision. They resisted direct authority. This was a big departure from the norms of the Matures' generation.

How Matures give and expect instruction at work:

> *"Place this widget in that box, then get Y tape so we can ship it."*

What they think and say:

> *"I'll do that now."*

How Boomers and Gen X give and prefer instructions:

"When you get a chance, could you see if we have some Y tape to seal up that part in a box so we can ship it please?"

What Boomers think and say:

"No problem. I'll do that today."

What Gen X thinks and says:

Thinks: *"You know I have an MBA. Can't we outsource this kind of stuff? I'll do it now so I can get back to my real work."*
Says: *"Sure thing."*

As you can see, about the only difference between these generations is a slightly different attitude toward how meaningful or important their work should be, but otherwise, the outward communication and actions are very similar.

Applying the Golden Rule, Boomers and Gen X have been attempting to give instruction to Gen Y and Gen Z the same way they want to receive it. But when instructions are given in the open and non-restrictive Boomer/Gen X language, things get lost in translation.

What Boomer and Gen X managers say:

"When you get a chance, could you see if we have some Y tape to seal up that part in a box so we can ship it please?"

What Gen Y thinks:

> *"Put the widgets in the boxes if you can find them. If not, ask for help. Tape will be required, so if we have Y tape, use it, but if not, ask for help. This can be done when you feel like it. It's not urgent."*

What Gen Z thinks:

> *"Widgets. Boxes. Tape. OK. Who uses widgets? Why aren't the boxes self-sealing? I'm going to order some self-sealing boxes, and if I can't, I'm going to patent that idea. I need to research the existing patents online. I'll get to the widgets after that."*

As you can see, different generational experiences as well as different life stages impact how directions are understood. The resulting Gen Y behaviors can be criticized as "needy," and the Gen Z behavior can be labeled as "undisciplined." The truth is it is simply misunderstanding. The suggestions below may be more effective, at least in the early stages of managing a new, younger employee.

A better way to instruct young employees:

> *"Place these widgets in those boxes, then get Y tape from the work room to seal it by 5 p.m. today for shipping. If you encounter any obstacles that could delay the shipment, please let me know as soon as possible. Once you've been through the process, see if you can spot opportunities to do this faster, cheaper, or better by changing the*

processes or materials we currently use, and let me know your thoughts by Monday."

Gen Y and Gen Z are both accustomed to completing tasks quickly, so they don't always have a sense of urgency to start a task, particularly if it seems boring. (Let's face it; any generation can be good at procrastinating unpleasant tasks.) For this reason, it is important that you are clear and specific on deadlines and deliverables. If you are clear on your timelines and expectations, they will do everything in their power to make you happy, including coming up with some great new ideas to improve your processes and reduce your costs. But also, be clear if you want new ideas to be run by you before they are implemented, because Gen Z might not realize this.

Like any new employee, your younger workers will need clear instructions and feedback until they are confident in their roles. Once they are confident, they are extremely high performers.

Managing Meetings by Generation

Meetings are the biggest time-waster at work for all generations.[30] But adapting meeting formats to the generational needs of your employees can help minimize some of this impact.

Gen Y looks much like the Boomers before them in their preference for group discussions and collaborative problem-solving in meetings. Gen X was much maligned by the

---

30 A. Gouveia, "2013 Wasting Time at Work Survey," *Salary.com*, March 19, 2014, accessed July 5, 2017, http://www.salary.com/2013-wasting-time-at-work-survey/.

Boomers for being anti-social in a workplace where Boomers had invented "Management by Walking Around." Gen Z seems more like their Gen X predecessors in this regard, preferring to only meet when necessary. As a result, meetings and collaboration will look different with the different generations. However, compared to Boomers and Gen X, your young employees are much more likely to tolerate or even prefer virtual discussions over in-person meetings.

Gen Y, and even more so Gen Z, are less likely to have longer, scheduled meetings and more likely to have ongoing GroupMe or WhatsApp discussion groups—where the group collaborates on questions and problems in real time. I have noticed that Gen X and Boomer employees can quickly get overwhelmed by having what seems like never-ending, large-scale, ongoing discussions rather than scheduled meetings. Below is a summary of what each generation thinks and does when they are assigned to a team project.

Manager: I'd like all of you to work on a launch event for our new product line. We'll need a full plan with timelines, budgets, vendors, and processes by the end of next month.

Boomer response: Let's all meet to brainstorm how we want to approach this, decide who's responsible for what, and schedule milestone meetings to keep us on track.

Gen X response: Let me know which part you want me to take care of, and I'll get it done.

Gen Y response: Let's do an off-site meeting at a restaurant so we can get to know each other, figure out what each of us is interested in doing, and then we can divide the work and keep each other posted on GroupMe. I can create a shared folder on Google Drive and invite everyone to collaborate.

Gen Z response: I've just formed a WhatsApp chat group so we can share ideas and information as we get it. Some of you didn't seem to be on WhatsApp yet, so I sent you invitations that you need to accept after you download the app. Once everyone's online, we can divide the work and schedule a Skype call if necessary to touch base. Who's up for Happy Hour?

As you can see, each generation has different expectations for how meetings and collaboration will work. You will get the best results using a hybrid approach that is established in the beginning to meet everyone's needs.

1. Ensure time for team-building that includes food or a fun activity to include Millennials. One of my favorites is to start every meeting with each person having 15 seconds to share one good thing that has happened to them since the last meeting. Use a timer for this activity.
2. Allow for independent work by establishing clear roles and responsibilities to ensure Gen Y and Gen Z know the limits.
3. Allow a tool for real-time discussion, such as GroupMe or WhatsApp, but establish limits around how and when it is to be used.

My Young Employee Won't Pick Up the Phone

Your young employees are happy to collaborate, but how they view collaboration may be different from how you view it. More importantly, both Gen Y and Gen Z are extremely unlikely to pick up the phone and call someone if they need to have a discussion.

They are as comfortable, if not more comfortable, e-mailing and texting than they are with communicating by telephone.

I have surveyed tens of thousands of young people for more than a decade about their communication preferences. It's a moving target, but since they are your customers as well as your employees, it's in your best interest to keep up. For instance, looking at responses from more than 3,000 students participating in my surveys in 2011, and again in 2016-2017, when asked "Which of the following media do you use for *frequent* and *regular* communication?," the percentage of responses broke out as follows:

	2016-2017 (Gen Z)	2011 (Gen Y)
Texting	82%	84%
E-mail	79%	82%
Facebook	72%	82%
Snapchat	66%	Not mentioned
Telephone	62%	58%
Instagram	54%	Not mentioned
LinkedIn	47%	Not mentioned
Twitter	33%	19%

Source: Belinne 2017, "2011, 2016, 2017 GENB Student Surveys, Survey Results."

As you can see, while both Gen Y and Gen Z are heavy users of technology in communication, the variety and type of media used for communication with the current generation is rapidly expanding. Is your company prepared to work with them on the platforms where they are already living and working, or do you expect them to adapt to older communication methods? If you expect them to adapt, are you willing to provide some guidance in best practices with telephone and e-mail etiquette?

Many employers complain that their young employees don't know how to leave a voicemail message or answer the phone professionally. These are learned skills that previous generations learned on their home telephones. This generation doesn't have a home telephone, so it is a skill that may need to be taught. Basic guidelines on telephone etiquette, while they may seem obvious to generations raised on "dumb" phones, are often necessary for smart phone generations. The basic expectations I outline for my young employees when using the telephone include:

1. Always answer the phone with "Hello, this is (your name)" rather than assuming they already know.
2. When leaving a message, clearly and slowly give your name and phone number (rather than assuming caller ID will take care of that) and your purpose for calling.
3. Always say "good bye" and generally say "thank you" before you hang up.

Case Study: Gen Y and the Teleconference Hang-up
Recently, I had a team of students working on a class project with a major corporation. The corporate leader for the

project hosted a teleconference to talk with the team. After their meeting, he called me to say that he had been explaining some finer points of the project when he realized all of the students had left the call. He reached out to the student leader to ask what happened, and the student told him the conference call shut down when they reached the one hour mark, so they all hung up and went about their days. The student said it never occurred to them to reach out to the corporate leader to let him know what had happened or to try to reschedule.

When I followed up with the students, it was clear they saw the corporate leader as being the person actually in charge, and therefore they assumed any outreach, change of plans, or rescheduling would be initiated by him. The good news is that with some coaching, the students better understood the expectations, and it never happened again.

Case Study: The Videoconference, the Boomer, and the Deodorant
I was in a videoconference recently with a diverse group of business leaders. As with most videoconference technology, participants had the option to mute the audio and/or video coming from their sites to the group. I watched as one member muted her audio. But clearly she thought she'd muted her video, because she proceeded to pull out a stick of deodorant, put it down the neck of her blouse, and apply it while the videoconference continued to take place. The lesson? Do not assume all your employees are comfortable with new technology when you launch it in your workplace.

Best Practices in Communication

1. Model good communication skills for young employees and, if necessary, set guidelines for professional communication.
2. Leverage the natural gifts of Gen Y to give visually attractive presentations and of Gen Z to use virtual technology and video in presentations.
3. Give clear and specific instructions with defined timelines, deliverables, and limits, but encourage feedback on processes from young employees.
4. Allow for group interactions that combine both in-person bonding time as well as virtual tools for real-time problem-solving and discussion.

CHAPTER 4

PRODUCTIVITY

I had a Gen Z student in my office the other day complaining that his job search wasn't going well. He'd had six interviews with good companies and two offers from his interviews so far. The job offers weren't quite in line with his goals, but they indicated he was on the right track with his search. This left me asking why he was coming to me for assistance. He answered, "Because I've been looking for two whole months, and I should have gotten the job I want by now!"

I told this student I was seeing most job searches in his field and industry taking about six months, which shocked him. We worked together to develop a detailed timeline for his search using milestones with shorter time horizons to help him stay focused and motivated. Once we broke the longer timeline into shorter chunks of activity, he was much more willing to be patient and stay on task.

Growing up in the age of immediate gratification has impacted the expectations and behavior of young employees, and these types of generational differences contribute to the challenge of managing their performance.

My Young Employee Can't Stay on Task

Per the Centers for Disease Control and Prevention, more than 10% of children ages 5-17 were diagnosed with ADHD between 2013 and 2015.[31] This compares to only 7.8% of children just 10 years earlier in 2003.[32] According to some studies, rates of ADHD diagnosis increased an average of 3% per year from 1997 to 2006.[33] Basically, the inability to focus and remain still for long periods of time is becoming more commonplace with each generation. But sometimes work requires focus, so how do you handle the young employee who has difficulty staying on task?

There is a great deal of brain research showing occasional distractions and taking time to move your brain from a focused task to a completely different and unfocused task can increase creativity and problem-solving skills.

According to a 2015 BrightHR study, 79% of young employees think fun at work is important, and nearly half think

---

31 Susanna N. Visser, Melissa L. Danielson, Rebecca H. Bitsko, Joseph R. Holbrook, Michael D. Kogan, Reem M. Ghandour, Ruth Perou, and Stephen J. Blumberg, "Trends in the Parent-Report of Health Care Provider-Diagnosed and Medicated Attention-Deficit/Hyperactivity Disorder: United States, 2003-2011," *Journal of the American Academy of Child & Adolescent Psychiatry* 53, no. 1 (January 2014), accessed July 5, 2017, https://www.cdc.gov/ncbddd/adhd/features/key-findings-adhd72013.html.

32 Ibid.

33 L.J. Akinbami, X. Liu, P.N. Pastor, and C.A. Reuben, "Attention Deficit Hyperactivity Disorder Among Children Aged 5-17 Years in the United States, 1998-2009," *NCHS Data Brief* 70 (August 2011), accessed July 2017, https://www.cdc.gov/nchs/products/databriefs/db70.htm.

it improves their productivity.[34] But more importantly, when looking at employees who don't take much sick leave, nearly two-thirds say they have fun at work.[35] This fun at work could be related to lower stress levels and therefore better health and lower absenteeism.

According to this same study, some of the activities to make work more fun included dress down days, office parties, pool tables, bringing pets to work, fantasy football, and even charitable fundraising. None of these programs need to be expensive or terribly distracting.

So, don't worry if your Gen Y or Gen Z employee sometimes decides to take a walk outside, watches a YouTube video, or sets up a game of paper football with the person in the cube across the hall. The real question is whether they are meeting their deadlines and deliverables. If they are, then these little breaks are helping them get their work done, and it's best not to interfere.

Thus, many companies offer walking trails, game rooms, gyms, and employee lounge areas that encourage young employees to take a mental break from complex tasks. When used appropriately, this can result in improved focus and creativity on the job as well as increased retention and commitment to the employer.

But what if your Gen Y or Gen Z employee is so distracted that he or she is not meeting deadlines and deliverables? This is the point where you need to try a different approach. I recently worked with a business owner who was having this exact problem. She had talked to the employee about performance expectations,

---

34 Sir Cary Cooper, "It Pays to Play," *BrightHR*, October 29, 2015, accessed July 5, 2017, https://pages.brighthr.com/itpaystoplay-v3.html.
35 Ibid.

but saw little behavior change, so I spoke to the employee as well. It turned out the manager and the employee had two very different perspectives.

Manager:

> *"[My young Gen Y employee] is attending school and preparing for a different career, so I know my position isn't his top priority, but it is still an important role in my company. Every time I walk by his office, he has his headphones on, and I'm not entirely sure if he's listening to music or listening to online classes. He also seems to be on social media every time I go by his office. In addition, he consistently breaks dress code and frequently comes to work late. But most importantly, he's having difficulty meeting deadlines, and his work often has many errors when he submits it.*
>
> *I've spoken to him about each of these things and how he's expected to be fully engaged while at work, to adhere to office policies, and to turn in timely and accurate work. He says that he understands, but nothing seems to change for more than a few days."*

Gen Y Employee:

> *"I am studying to do computer design, so I'm an artist. Music and computer visuals are interesting and relaxing for me. My job has me doing a bunch of data entry and spreadsheets, so the music and the social media helps me unwind when the details start to stress me out. There's a lot of stressful data entry, so I need a lot of unwinding to balance that out.*

As for the dress code, I'm not meeting with key clients, so it seems kind of stupid for me to have to put on slacks and a dress shirt every day when nobody sees me but other people in the office. It's a stupid rule, so the only way we'll ever change the rule is if somebody pushes back on it, so I'm just steadily pushing back until we get a change. The same thing with the showing up on time and arbitrary report deadlines. It shouldn't matter if I'm a little late if I'm willing to make up the time or if the report isn't mission critical.

I don't get why older managers are always enforcing rules just for the sake of being uptight and controlling. I don't do well in that type of environment. As for the errors on the reports, there aren't that many, and my reports go through about three approval processes, so I know there's somebody double-checking my work for me. "

The manager and the employee clearly have very different mindsets. Working with each of them, we were able to resolve all of their issues by helping to establish a shared understanding of the behaviors and goals that best meet both of their needs.

1. **Headphones and social media**

    We decided to institute the Pomodoro technique (by Francesco Cirillo) where he would set a timer to work uninterrupted on a project for 25 minutes and then take five minutes to explore online. We agreed that the employee could listen to music while working as long as reports were accurate and on time. If music truly helps his focus, he can prove this by improving his accuracy while listening to music. However, if the accuracy doesn't improve, then it may be an indicator that the music is more of a distraction than a help.

2. **Dress code**

The approach to this was twofold. First, I reframed the concept of dress code for the employee. He was perceiving it as a means of arbitrary control. I asked him when he went on a date if he was dressing up for himself or for his date. He said he dressed up for his date. I said this was the same thing. We put some time into our appearance at work as a way of showing respect for our customers and our co-workers. It's basically how we show that the other people are worth the trouble. Once he saw the dress code as a way to support the people around him, he never came to work looking like he'd just rolled out of bed again.

Next, I told him that when I was a young employee, I was required to wear skirts, pantyhose, and heels to work every day. But then I explained that I haven't worn pantyhose in more than ten years, nor do I require it of my employees. I said that I worked within the system to prove I could do the work "their way" until I earned a promotion, and then when I was the leader, I was able to change the rules. I told him if he could demonstrate his ability to be successful within the existing constraints, then when he was promoted to leadership, he could change the rules, too. But if he couldn't work within the constraints, the only thing people would notice is his rebellion, and nobody would see his competency, so he'd be limiting not only his career growth, but his ability to affect real change in the future. He understood that concept.

3. **Timeliness**

   I pointed out that when he was late, everyone else was either forced to cover for him or put under time pressure to make up for his delay. He didn't like the idea of inconveniencing his peers. Then I explained how, even if he was the most brilliant person ever to have a job, if he's consistently late, people will be too busy being annoyed by the inconvenience to notice how good he is.

In general, young employees are easier to manage when expectations are clear and tied to both team success and a higher purpose. But when it comes to productivity, the internet is still one of the biggest distractions in the workplace, so it deserves a more in-depth discussion as a specific challenge in performance management.

Managing Mobile and Internet Use at Work

"She can't go for more than a minute without checking her phone."

"Every time I walk by his desk, he's on Facebook."

"I don't understand why he can't just pick up the phone and call me."

"I'm in the office next to hers and she still instant messages me."

I've heard comments like these made about members of every generation in the workplace at one time or another. "Phone addiction" is an epidemic in the workplace as well as our society. The younger generations are simply more native to the internet and mobile technology than the older generations.

Gen Y grew up with multitasking parents who were on Blackberries (called "Crackberries" at the time) during their play dates at the park or on cell phones for work meetings during soccer practice. As a result, they generally don't feel rude or uncomfortable using technology while interacting with others at work. For them, multitasking mobile communication with interpersonal communication is normal and expected. If you don't want them to do this in the work place, you must not only explicitly tell them that it is not acceptable behavior, *but you must also make sure that the rest of your workplace models good cell phone etiquette.*

Along these lines, many managers have expressed concern that the current generation spends too much time online doing non-work activities while at work. As a result, a variety of internet blocking and social media policies have appeared around the country. In the past, we simply didn't have the opportunity or the means to waste time at work as effectively as we do now.

If you look at the major technological advances in the workplace for the previous generations, you'll notice that the current generation of technology is, hands down, the most distracting.

Generation	Technological Change
Boomers	Fax machines, photocopiers, computers
Gen X	Internet, cell phones, videoconference
Gen Y	Social media, smart phones, Skype
Gen Z	Instagram, Snapchat, GroupMe

It's easy to make assumptions about the younger generations wasting time on the internet, and otherwise getting easily
distracted from work, since these are areas where they've had an
earlier start in life. But according to a recent Salary.com survey,
that's not the case. In fact, employees in the 18-25 age bracket
were the *least* likely to waste time on the internet while at work.[36]

Time Wasted at Work by Age

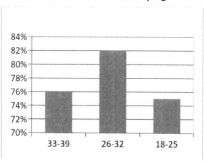

Source: Gouveia 2014

---

36 A. Gouveia, "2013 Wasting Time at Work Survey," *Salary.com*, March 19,
2014, accessed July 5, 2017, http://www.salary.com/2013-wasting-time-at-work-
survey/.

The same survey showed that about one-third of all workers admit to wasting time on the internet daily, so it does have a cost to employers in terms of lost productivity.[37]

Impact of Social Media/Internet Use at Work

Although the internet presents a challenge, there are also some very important reasons to consider leaving it open and accessible to all employees at work.

- Younger generations, in particular, are accustomed to work-life integration, rather than work-life balance. So while they use the internet at work for some personal use, they will also use the internet at home for work. In that sense, it evens out over time.
- Social media is the modern "water cooler." A certain amount of socializing at work keeps employees happy and engaged in the workplace.
- Social media can also be a networking forum where young professionals can learn from other professionals without charging the company association and meeting fees.
- Strict internet and social media policies make it harder to recruit and retain young workers, who are accustomed to open and immediate access to information. Some would argue overly strict policies could also stunt creativity, in that a quick surf on the internet may unlock creative ideas in the same way a quick walk around the building was once encouraged.

---

37   Ibid.

- If you lock down their computers, they'll just use their phones and tablets. You can't really stop online access while at work.

There are also many good reasons to consider having internet and social media policies in place at your office.

- 70% of porn is viewed between 9 a.m. and 5 p.m. at work.[38]
- Across a variety of surveys, it is estimated that the total cost of surfing on work time in the US is well over $130B.
- Privacy and security are more easily compromised with unrestricted access to the internet.
- Your employees are representing your brand, even when they are on their personal social media sites.

Your employees will surf on work time if they choose to do so, regardless of your policies and firewalls. You must not only try to minimize the time spent doing this, but also make sure that when they do so, your company's brand is protected.

Establishing Effective Social Media and Internet Policies

Your organization should have a social media and internet policy. *The best approach is to involve your employees in creating the guidelines.* Make sure it is a diverse team in terms of

---

38 C. Conner, "Who Wastes the Most Time at Work?" *Forbes*, September 7, 2013, accessed July 5, 2017, http://www.forbes.com/sites/cherylsnappconner/2013/09/07/who-wastes-the-most-time-at-work/.

generation and attitudes toward technology, and give them clear goals for the policies. Remember that Gen Y and Gen Z are used to being included in major decisions, and they are likely more aware of recent privacy issues and loopholes than you are. Leverage their experience and knowledge by giving them key places in these policy committees. They won't let you down, and they will bring you a fresh perspective that can safely carry your policies into the next decade.

Some recommended goals might include:

- Ensuring employee posts are not discriminatory, inflammatory, or libelous
- Clarifying how posts should never damage the company brand or share confidential/insider information
- Defining how to separate an employee's personal brand from the corporate brand online
- Preventing online altercations outside of work with co-workers or customers
- Limiting the company's exposure to negative media coverage due to social media use by employees
- Ensuring company property and networks are not used to access inappropriate, illegal, inflammatory, or pornographic materials
- Defining privacy when using company computers and networks: How much personal work can be done using company equipment? How much e-mail or file privacy can an employee expect when using corporate networks and equipment?
- Minimizing the company's exposure to hackers and viruses

- Clarifying privacy expectations for communications sent or received on the company's behalf
- Maximizing workplace productivity

Not all time lost at work is due to personal surfing or social media. Most would agree that work e-mail has a way of consuming our days and impeding our output. There are many excellent techniques and programs available to help your employees better manage their e-mail so they can remain productive. The approach you use will depend on the needs of your office. However, investing in effective e-mail management training for your team will generally pay high dividends in employee morale and productivity.

Helping Your Young Employee Manage Others

I recently worked with an area leader (a Gen Y manager for a sandwich chain) who shared the following issues with me:

> *"I have two employees I can tell want raises and promotions, and I really like them, but the truth is they're not always reliable or flexible with me, which makes it hard for me to justify giving them more money or a higher title. At the same time, they haven't told me directly that they want more, they've just dropped hints, so I'm not sure I should even open that can of worms."*

First, it's useful to note that Gen Y was not raised in an environment that encouraged constructive conflict, so it's not uncommon to see these types of conflict-avoidant situations.

As a result, direct confrontation needs to be handled carefully. I asked the Gen Y manager how he currently handled performance situations, and he said that when his employees weren't at their best, he would usually bring them to sit outside with him one-on-one so he could tell them about the things they were doing that he liked, in order to reward and encourage more good behavior.

There's a lot to be said for the "Catch Them Doing Something Right" philosophy of Gen Y management. Because he was regularly praising good behavior, he'd built up a goodwill account he could cash in when giving constructive feedback. At the same time, if you never have that honest conversation with someone about what it takes to get to the next level, they will continue to feel overlooked and underappreciated until they quit their job in frustration.

I asked the manager specifically what problems existed with the employees, and he said that one person, because she was a single mother, always had to leave at exactly 3:00 to pick up her child. She wants to be promoted to a management role, but because the manager sometimes has to cover for absent employees, that person must have more flexibility than she does. But he was scared it would be inappropriate or even illegal to say something like that to a single mother. The other employee had a problem with ongoing tardiness, but he knows this employee wants and needs more money to pay for school. The manager quickly went on to excuse the behavior as being *"not that late, just 10 to 15 minutes every day, but still late. And it's not really his fault because he's in school and always exhausted. I don't want to discourage him from working hard at school by giving him a hard time about this."*

As a Gen Y manager who values inclusiveness, balance, and encouragement, confronting employees with problematic behaviors didn't fit his natural definition of good leadership.

So as a way to respect everyone's beliefs and cultural needs, while still making the business a priority, we came up with the following solution.

The Gen Y manager no longer pulls people outside randomly to tell them what they're doing right. He compliments good performance immediately when he sees it on the job, and he schedules monthly one-on-one meetings with his direct reports to go over their accomplishments, goals, and obstacles—first from *their* perspective and then from *his*. By starting with accomplishments, he can acknowledge their contributions and build the goodwill account. Because goals are next, he can see if they actually want to be on the management track, or if they are just planning to do the job until they graduate or find something else.

Because he manages sandwich shops, he's better off creating a safe, open dialogue where employees can talk about their plans to leave, if they have them, so he can plan around it. Also, the development plan and expectations for someone who sees the job as temporary will be different from someone who sees the job as a growth opportunity.

For the employees who want to be promoted to manager, we decided that the Gen Y leader should use the one-on-one meetings to ask them what they see as preventing them from succeeding. He would also take this opportunity to advise his employees on the areas where they could benefit from experience and growth, while working with them to outline a plan for developing the necessary skills and experiences to move into management. Ultimately, we agreed that this needs to be done in a collaborative, joint problem-solving manner.

For instance, let's look at the single mother. The fact that her schedule is inflexible is directly tied to her ability to meet the expectations of the manager role, and it's only fair to open that conversation if she wants to be promoted to management. Now let's examine how the manager might approach this conversation.

Employee: *I'd like to be a manager one day, but even though I've worked here a long time, I never get promoted.*

Manager: *I'd like to see you become a manager one day, too. You've been a great employee, and I'd like to see you stay and grow here. One of the expectations of the manager role is that you be able to take on extra shifts on short notice if we are short-staffed. What would be your plan for handling that?*

Notice that her 3:00 leave time or her status as a mother wasn't part of the discussion. The manager stayed focused on her potential and the expectations of the role. Then he involved the employee in joint problem-solving. This generation believes strongly in work-life balance, and successful managers will respect that by being open to creative solutions that meet the needs of both the employee and the business.

The other employee issue we needed to resolve was the chronically tardy student who wants more money. It's entirely possible that this person doesn't want to be a manager, but the tardiness still needs to be addressed. Again, let's take a look at how the manager might approach this.

Employee*: I plan to work here until I graduate college, and then I'll try to find something that fits with my major. I appreciate* *how flexible you've been with my study schedule, but I really need more money to pay for school.*

Manager: *I'm glad you have plans for the future, and I'm also glad we can be part of helping you reach your goals. I know it can be very overwhelming to balance work and school, and it seems that sometimes you're so overworked and overtired that you have trouble getting to work on time. Unfortunately, when that happens, your co-workers have to cover for you until you arrive, which puts them in a bad spot as well. Given that your work has been strong in every other area, I think if we could fully resolve the timeliness issue, we could look at a salary increase in the next six months. What suggestions do you have for helping you get to work on time consistently?*

Again, it's important to respect the fact that the young employee has life goals outside of work. The more open you are in discussions about this, the less likely they are to suddenly quit on short notice. However, you also need to meet the needs of the business. Helping your Gen Y or Gen Z employee understand how bad behavior at work hurts their co-workers is more likely to get their attention than bringing up how it hurts the business. They tend to be more loyal to people than to brands, particularly those who are just performing a job rather than pursuing a calling.

Best Practices in Productivity Management

1. Set clear and reasonable expectations for breaks and play time during the work day. (Work together on a plan that meets both parties' needs.)

2. Establish social media and internet policies that protect your company without stifling employee freedom and creativity.

3. Help young employees see how their productivity personally impacts co-workers and customers.

4. Catch employees doing something right—recognize and reward good behavior as it happens as often as possible to make constructive criticism more likely to be heard.

5. Meet individually on a regular basis to discuss achievements, goals, and obstacles with each employee, first from their perspective and then from yours.

CHAPTER 5

MOTIVATION

The other day, I met with a Gen Y employee who had always worked in customer service prior to taking his first "real" job as an analyst at a major corporation. When I asked him how things were going, he said it was harder than he'd anticipated to spend his days crunching numbers and converting spreadsheets to PowerPoint presentations. He then added, *"The only thing that's keeping me sane is the fact that they have a basketball court and a PlayStation set up for when we just have to clear our heads."* I asked him if the games were a distraction and if they interfered with him getting his work done on time, and he replied, *"Those little breaks are the only things that help me clear my head enough to really focus on my work, so I don't start getting tired and sloppy."*

His experience is actually supported by research showing that breaks improve focus.[39] While younger generations

39 Atsunori Ariga and Alejandro Lleras, "Brief and Rare Mental 'Breaks' Keep You Focused: Deactivation and Reactivation of Task Goals Preempt Vigilance Decrements," *Cognition* 118, no. 3 (March 2011), doi: 10.1016/j. cognition.2010.12.007.

are often criticized for bringing things like basketball and PlayStations to the workplace, these types of programs may help employees of all generations be more productive.

Simple and Effective Recognition Programs

While it was the Boomers who started the "I'm OK, You're OK Too" movement, and the Gen X helicopter parents who ensured their children were consistently praised and recognized, these generations were also the first managers to complain when Gen Y entered the workforce seeking frequent praise and recognition for their work. Yet employees who want to please and impress their managers can be your best employees. We need to continue to grow and develop this wonderful generation of young, confident, and optimistic professionals. But how?

More Trophies with Little Time or Money

Yes, Gen Y needs recognition. To be honest, though, your entire workforce, regardless of generation, can benefit from recognition programs—and they don't need to be expensive. In my own research, I've found that Gen Y are more motivated by being given opportunities for growth and recognition than they are by money. Don't get me wrong; they like money, too. It's just not the primary motivator for this generation. Therefore, even if you can't develop cash incentives, you can still have a motivated and engaged workforce.

Never underestimate the power of a high five, or a simple "good job" for any employee. Depending on their personality, they may prefer recognition at a meeting or a personal e-mail of appreciation from a manager. As a manager, the more you can notice and adapt to their individual recognition preferences, the more effectively you can motivate your team, regardless of generation. There are some trends regarding younger generations, and you can use these insights to help shape your recognition programs.

For example, the younger generations post every accomplishment online, ideally as a picture. But this phenomenon isn't unique to Gen Y or Gen Z. It's just been fine-tuned and perfected by them. So your best recognition programs are the ones that are photo-worthy. Since these generations are highly motivated by collaborative work, peer-to-peer recognition programs are excellent. And because they are focused on pleasing the authority figure in their offices as well, managerial recognition is also critical. So beyond the usual "good job," how can we motivate and recognize our high-performing Gen Y and Gen Z employees? There are several ways, and none are particularly expensive in terms of time or money.

1. **Develop peer-to-peer recognition programs**. These are programs where a co-worker formally recognizes an employee for good work or assistance, and the recognition is routed through the employee's manager for signature before being given to the employee. I've seen this used effectively in several offices, and most employees post their recognition notes all over their work space. I have also seen some workplaces where employees are entered into periodic prize drawings, with one entry for each appreciation card received.

2. **Post an acknowledgment board**. Ideally, this is placed in the employee break area where co-workers or managers can recognize people who complete projects or provide extraordinary help on a problem. Encourage managers to help keep the board full, with posts lasting about a week.

3. **Post individual or group photos of recognized staff members on the company's social media**. If you allow the employees to repost to their own pages, it has the added benefit of building your company's brand as a supportive work environment.

4. **Open meetings with celebration time**. Give each person 30 seconds (use a timer) to say one good thing they accomplished since the last meeting—whether it's on the project, at work, or in their personal lives.

5. **Have fun**. After major projects, if possible, schedule fun days at the office where employees can dress "picnic casual," bring their pets to work, or have a scheduled movie time during a long lunch break. Simple things like this are a great way to show you recognize that a particular project or deadline has really pushed your team hard. More than anything, Gen Y and Gen Z want to have fun at work, because they plan to work a lot. The analytics company SAS is consistently named one of the top places to work. There are many reasons for this, but among them is the fact that SAS is the top corporate purchaser of M&Ms in the world. Why? Because they offer unlimited M&Ms to their employees at work. How simple is that?

6. **Offer more team competitions than individual competitions**. Whereas Gen X responded well to individual incentive programs, Gen Y and Gen Z are more accustomed to team competitions, and they will work hard to motivate and build their teammates. They don't have to just be work-based, either. I've had cross-functional teams play Jeopardy-style trivia games to learn about the organization's history, and they've not only been great team builders, but also great learning opportunities. Sports teams, bowling outings, and other non-work team activities can be great ways to build loyalty and improve internal communication. Some of my most effective strategic planning meetings have alternated planning time with fun activity throughout the day to keep people creative and open.

Retention Programs

You know it's important to help all of your employees see meaning in their work. But Gen Y and Gen Z in particular need to understand how their work ties into not only the goals of the company, but also to a higher purpose and meaning in the world. Bear in mind that Gen Y is the generation that fully developed the concept of "Social Entrepreneurship." They have been building businesses to make a difference since they were children. They've raised thousands of dollars through GoFundMe and other crowdsourcing sites, but they seldom paid themselves a salary.

I've surveyed thousands of Gen Y in my work, and consistently their top motivator is "opportunities for advancement and learning." Finding a "higher purpose" in their work is always toward the top of the list as well. While high salary is still important to them, as a generation, they are more focused on fulfillment than cash. A successful company will provide both a fair salary and meaningful growth for its employees, and it doesn't have to be difficult. This will become even more important as Gen Z enters the workplace, since they are more aware, involved, and active in social causes than any previous generation was at their age.

There are many effective, inexpensive tools to keep employees engaged. Let's take a look at a few of them:

1. **Help employees see the company's higher purpose and their role in it**. For example, your Gen Y employee isn't just doing an audit. She's protecting companies and the economy from fraud, and by extension, she's protecting jobs and families. Your Gen Z isn't just designing a bridge, she's creating a way to safely connect families to one another, and people to job opportunities that wouldn't be possible without her work. Every time one of my career counselors tells me about helping a student, at the end of my praise to them, I say, "Your work changed his life for the better." I should add that I have an incredibly effective, productive, and motivated team, with very little turnover, because they all know in their hearts that their work improves lives.

2. **Increase their responsibility**. Don't just pile on work without pay and act like that's a compliment. Slowly broaden the scope of their authority and responsibility, and make it clear it's because they've earned your trust and confidence. Then, if they get the results, by all means, make sure you pay them fairly for their outcomes.

3. **Have succession plans and clear promotion tracks**. When employees understand the path they can follow to move up, they will rise to the occasion. If they believe their job is a dead end, they will not only be less productive at work, but they will also be more likely to leave you for a competitor. One of the main reasons young employees leave an employer is because they don't see clear opportunities for growth in their company.

4. **Have online training**. Gen Y expects to be given instructions on how best to succeed in your organization. While Gen Z is good at "figuring it out" on their own, they may not always figure out precisely how your organization likes to do things. For this reason, it's best to have formal training which is ideally online and self-paced. Simulations and interactive, online training, in particular, are effective. In other words, after the initial investment, training does not need to be expensive. Webinars, webcasts, and podcasts are simple and inexpensive to create, and they will get more use and results than training manuals. Of course, the training should still be high quality and visually stimulating to be effective.

5. **Offer rotational programs**. Because most young people, regardless of generation, are still deciding where they fit in the world of work, rotational programs have the added benefit of helping new employees see the big picture of your organization while increasing retention and career focus. The more organized and defined these are, the better. The best programs typically have six-month rotations through three or four divisions before the employee and the company mutually select a final placement.

6. **Offer mentor programs**. Gen Y and Gen Z both respond very well to training and mentoring. Both groups need to feel connected to and valued by more experienced people in the organization. New employees benefit from guidance on navigating the political landscape of an organization, since corporate America operates very differently from schools and universities. We cover more information on mentor programs in Chapter 6, "Recruiting."

7. **Offer inclusiveness programs**. Our country becomes more diverse each year, with Gen Z being the most diverse generation in history. These generations assume diversity, and they embrace it completely. They love groups and activities that bring people together to celebrate our differences and similarities. Allowing them to connect with others in the organization who have similar backgrounds or interests will improve both morale and retention. It can be as simple as a walking group at lunch or a monthly book club. Depending on the size of

your company, groups for LGBT, racial and ethnic minorities, or women may also be valued as a
resource for focused presentations or programs,
bringing together a diverse group of people in the
company to better understand the perspectives
and culture of a particular affinity group.

While recognition, growth, and purpose are critical to the
motivation and engagement of employees, Gen Y and Gen
Z—even more than Gen X before them—want *flexibility*.
They receive a great deal of criticism for this from their employers, so the topic deserves further discussion.

The Flexible and Productive Workplace

In my surveys of thousands of young people, the desire for
flexibility is always a common theme. The most common corporate resistance to this is the idea that people will be less
productive if they are not all in the same place at the same
time. But with current communication tools, it is seldom as
necessary for someone to be physically present to be effective
at work as it was in past decades.

As a leader and as an HR manager, I did a great deal of
experimenting with mommy-track, job sharing, flex schedules, and telecommuting. My personal experience, and the
experience of other managers with whom I've talked, is if
you set clear expectations on outcomes and communication,
staff members who are given these options are significantly
more productive on their flexible schedules than they are on
traditional schedules.

Case Study: Mommy-Track Contractor
Several years ago, I heard from one of my former MBA
students who had moved to Houston. She was a brilliant
and talented MBA, but as a mother of four, she and her
husband had decided to focus on his career, and she had
followed him around the world as a trailing spouse. When
she arrived in Houston, she wanted to work, but it needed
to be completely flexible, part-time work she could do on
her own schedule from home, while ideally taking advantage of her project management and corporate communications experience.

As luck would have it, I had just come up with the
idea to start an experiential component in a large course
I was teaching. In this course, teams of sophomore-level
students would spend the semester working on simple
research projects for corporations and non-profits in the
area. I didn't have the bandwidth to manage this, though,
so I hired her as a contractor to manage the program. I
gave her the vision, the constraints, some leads, targets,
and deadlines. And she exceeded all expectations. In the
first semester, we brought in 20 companies to work with
160 students, and we received national recognition for the
program almost immediately.

Over time, she refined and defined the program to the
point that it now comprises 40 projects each semester with
well over 300 students. For a period, her husband was re-
located to San Francisco, but she continued to manage the
program for me, and none of our project sponsors or students ever realized that she wasn't in Houston. The communications processes remained seamless. The key to this type

of work arrangement is having clear expectations and deliverables and paying for outcomes, not time.

Case Study: Job Sharing

When I was working in human resources, one of my best HRIS employees had her first child and asked me if she could move to part time rather than quitting. There was no doubt in my mind that I was better off with 50% of an excellent, experienced employee than 100% of a new employee. At the same time, she still had at least 40 hours of work that needed to be accomplished each week.

The job sharing concept met with more resistance than you'd think, given that I worked in HR, but I finally was able to create a program to hire another half-time person to job share with her. The experienced employee handled the more complex part of the job, the new employee handled more of the paperwork, and the two shared a client base. I'm not going to say that sharing a client base was easy, and we did lose some productivity each day because they needed to spend time sharing information about cases.

However, they were both so appreciative to be given this type of flexible arrangement that they each accomplished more in 20 hours than most of my staff accomplished in 30. They were always incredibly focused and efficient on the job, and they were, by necessity, my most organized employees as well. The end result was an arrangement that was harder on them than it was on our organization, but they remained motivated and engaged due to their appreciation of the flexibility.

Do I Need to Convert to a Completely "Open" Work Environment?

I've seen lots of articles about how Gen Y wants completely open work environments, and I'm fairly certain these were all funded by companies that manufacture cubicles or other modular workstations.

I surveyed more than 5,000 Millennials over a three year period, and here's what they said about their preferences in terms of office environment:

Mix of open and private offices:	35%
Private offices preferred:	17%
Open format preferred:	16%
Telecommuting preferred:	12%
Work in the field:	11%
Indifferent:	9%

Source: Belinne 2017, "2010-2017 GENB Student Surveys, Survey Results."

As you can see, the preferences for office types are as diverse as the people who will inhabit them. More introverted employees still like the ability to go to a private or home office to focus, while more extroverted employees get their best ideas in open formats or in the field. But the majority of young employees fall somewhere in the middle, where they can both interact with co-workers as well as have private spaces free from distraction.

Where Gen Y differs from previous generations is in the idea that private offices are always necessary indicators of status and importance. Gen Y is more concerned about being in an environment that maximizes their individual productivity and work styles. Unless your company sets up its reward system such that only people at a certain level get private offices, then environments that offer a combination of team work areas as well as private work spaces to allow for focused concentration will work best.

Do I Have to Let Everyone Telecommute?

While Gen Y is often accused of only wanting to work from home, as you saw in the previous chart, the truth is that they tend to thrive in environments where they can work in teams, since that is how they were educated and raised. In talking to companies and employees, I've actually seen more Gen X employees requesting telecommuting arrangements than Gen Y.

I've even had several Gen Y and even some Gen Z students decide to leave jobs that were 100% telecommute because they didn't have the sense of community and support that they needed to feel connected to the company and positioned for growth.

With the most recent group of Gen Z students, however, there is a growing trend toward a preference for more telecommuting. Because this generation is digitally native, they are much more accustomed to working and interacting with others in a virtual setting, so they can get the same benefits of group camaraderie in a virtual environment that Gen Y needs in the office. You may find it more difficult to convince Gen Z employees of the need to come into the office for meetings or activities when those same activities could be accomplished virtually. They like to connect with their teammates, but not just for the sake of "face time" in the office.

Because the younger generations are very adept at working virtually, and even building close and meaningful relationships in a virtual setting, I would challenge you to consider if you need to require all employees to be physically present at all times. While some customer-facing roles definitely benefit from in-person meetings, and long or emotionally charged meetings can often be managed better in person, if you are managing by outcomes and objectives rather than face-time in the office, it is not always necessary for all employees to be physically present at all times.

Also, by allowing staff members to save time and money on daily commutes and professional dress, you can often win extra loyalty and commitment from both your young and more "seasoned" employees!

Telecommuting and Flex Schedules

My current teams are all customer-facing teams. They either serve corporations or they serve college students, and much of that work is done on-site in our offices. For this reason, I was hesitant to offer telecommuting. How do you serve customers if you're not in the office?

However, I started experimenting, at the request of my Gen X employees, and it has worked beautifully. I can't offer it when we have high demand for in-office services from customers, but we do quite a bit of telecommuting in the off-season. I have actually seen increases in productivity as a result.

Here are the guidelines that have made telecommuting more effective for my teams:

1. Entire teams can't be out on the same day.
2. Prior to working from home, employees and their managers will agree on which projects they will be working on and what deliverables can be expected.
3. Employees must be available to customers and managers by e-mail and phone during normal working hours.

The biggest concern for most managers is that productivity will decrease if they are not able to monitor their employees' work habits. While this may be true in some cases, if you are managing by deliverables and outcomes rather than face-time, you will have more productive employees, regardless of where they are working. However, if you give an employee the opportunity to avoid a brutal commute or give them the chance to wear their pajamas while they work from home, they can still be held to the same output standards while increasing their morale and loyalty.

Along the same lines, I encourage flexible schedules. Again, my teams are customer-facing, so I need to have people in the office. However, if some people want to work early schedules and some want to work late schedules, not only do I get to offer them a work schedule that meets their personal needs, but I also get to extend our total customer-facing hours. By allowing this flexibility, I get the added benefit of having staff coverage from early in the morning until the evening. So our customers love the arrangement as well. In addition, it's often easier for me to recruit new staff as well as retain existing staff because of the flexible arrangements I'm willing to offer.

I've often had other departmental leaders ask how I got my teams to keep our department open early mornings, late nights, and weekends. To which I always reply, "They asked to do it." Nobody ever believes me, but my experience has been that most people are very open to working odd hours if you are willing to work around their daughter's soccer practice, their morning cross fit group, or their Friday afternoon volunteer time at their son's school.

I have also offered 9-80 work weeks—where employees work nine-hour days, for a total of 80 hours over a two-week period, and then they take alternating Fridays or Mondays off. These generally didn't work particularly well in my departments, because my teams didn't like the days being scheduled for nine hours. However, I have seen them work extremely well with some of the companies for whom I've consulted. If the primary concern is that the 9-80 leaves the office vacant on Fridays, simply divide up the work teams so half of the team alternates Mondays off and the other half alternates Fridays off. One year, I had a woman who worked 10 hour days and took off every Wednesday. With flexible schedules, the emphasis is on being *flexible*.

If you offer a flexible workplace and your competitors don't, where do you think the best employees will want to work? In addition, if your employees are posting on their personal social media about how much they like your work-place policies, you can't buy better recruiting advertising than that!

Best Practices for Motivation

1. Tie the work of the employee and the work of the company to a higher purpose and meaning!
2. Focus more on outcomes than processes—be open to flexible schedules, telecommuting, and a mix of work and play in the office if goals and deadlines are being met.
3. Create an environment that encourages frequent individual and group recognition from both peers and managers.
4. Provide structured training and advancement programs for young employees so they can understand what is required to grow in the organization.

CHAPTER 6

RECRUITING

When Boomers and Gen X were graduating from college and beginning their careers, they generally checked newspaper classified ads or read job postings on a career center bulletin board to find a job. Now, with LinkedIn, web crawlers like Indeed.com, and thousands of corporate social media pages, it's difficult to get your message seen by the right candidates through all the online noise.

I've been hiring and placing college graduates for nearly three decades, and I can say without hesitation that the current generation is the least involved in the job search that I've ever seen—largely because they're completely overwhelmed by all the information available. I have worked for and with public and private universities, ranked and unranked programs, traditional universities and diversity colleges, but the challenges are similar across all of them.

Getting Their Attention

Over the years, I've surveyed thousands of college students to determine how they want a company to communicate with them, and here's what they told me by percentage selecting each option:

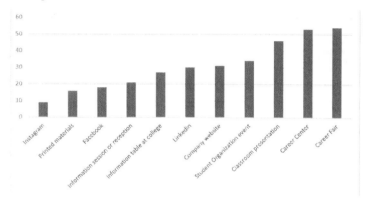

Source: Belinne 2017, "2010-2017 GENB Student Surveys, Survey Results."

As you can see, while they may be actively using things like Snapchat and Instagram, that's not where they want their recruiting to take place. More traditional channels that involve some level of relationship-building, whether directly with the student or with the college, are still the favorites. You may also notice that information sessions and receptions are not as popular as they were for previous generations. Current college students continue to be overscheduled with school, work, and extracurricular activities, leaving little extra time for scheduled events beyond their existing commitments.

With that said, the adage of "it's not what you know, but who you know," still rings true for both Gen Y and Gen Z.

They are more likely to show interest in a company if they know someone who works there than if they read about them online.

While online presence is good, taking the time to meet with college students and get to know them will put your organization ahead of its competitors in recruiting. The trick is to "meet them where they are" at things like student organization events and classroom presentations. I've seen students turn down larger paychecks and more "prestigious" companies just because they felt like the recruiters and hiring managers at a specific company cared about them as people. In the end, Gen Y and Gen Z are not that different from young employees in previous generations.

Lately, I am seeing more major employers move to virtual hiring platforms in an effort to reduce costs and increase diversity of the candidate pool. The irony is that my students who are racial and ethnic minorities are the ones most resistant to the virtual hiring process. They prefer developing a personal relationship with the recruiter and hiring managers to ensure they feel accepted and at home with the company. For this reason, it is critical to maintain a personal campus presence, even if the hiring platform will be virtual.

What They're Seeking in an Employer

I surveyed more than 3,000 young people over six years to measure differences in priorities when selecting new employers over time. The chart below shows the percentage selecting each priority by generation. (Respondents could select their top three choices.)

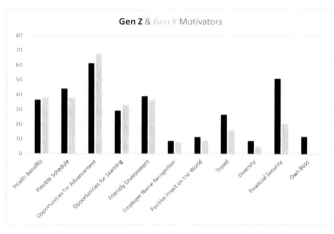

Source: Belinne 2017, "2010-2017 GENB Student Surveys, Survey Results."

As you can see, opportunities for advancement is consistently ranked at the top of the list as the most important quality in a future employer, regardless of generation. This is especially true for Gen Y who wants approval and growth within their companies as quickly as possible. The more your company can clearly explain the training, mentoring, professional development, and rotational programs you may offer, the better. In addition, clear career ladders with typical timelines and milestones for advancement will quickly make you a preferred employer.

One notable difference between Gen Z and Gen Y is that Gen Z is more focused on financial stability. They're also more likely to want to start their own businesses soon after graduation. Because Gen Y came of age during a period of relative financial stability in the US, they are less likely, as a generation, to worry about their long-term financial stability. Gen Z, by comparison, came of age during the Great Recession and spent their childhoods experiencing more scarcity and uncertainty than the previous generation. This experience has driven them not only to look at the stability of a company, but also to be more self-reliant when it comes to financial security.

To recruit Gen Z, companies will need to focus on how they are innovating and growing. Stories of young employees who have been given the opportunity to work on new technologies or product lines will appeal to Gen Z students.

I often get questions on these survey results about why "Diversity" scores so low when I keep saying that diversity is so important to the younger generation. I followed up with students to ask this question, and the response I consistently received is that diversity is assumed by this generation. In other words, they expect that your organization will naturally embrace diversity, so they don't see it as something they would need to actively seek. However, if you don't meet their expectations for diversity, they will not want to work for you, and they will tell their friends not to work for you.

Another survey option that seems surprising based on most generation research is how few selected "Positive Impact on the World" as a top priority. In speaking to students, this is another area where they assume it will happen based on the career choices they make. For instance, I had an accounting student tell me she loved audit, because she knew her work was protecting people's financial security from unnecessary risk and fraud. I had a supply chain student tell me he loved his major because he knew that a good supply chain not only helped create jobs around the world, but it allowed companies to provide more value and better products to people who needed them. In other words, students have already decided that their jobs will be meaningful, so it is your job as an organization to prove them right with your actions.

Like previous generations, young people often determine they will fit with a company because they like the people they have met from the organization, and they feel like their values align with the company's values. It is more important than ever that your company can clearly communicate its purpose and values, and that your employees live its purpose and values clearly. Students notice when all employees refer to the corporate mission or can give examples of how the company lives its values. The best companies have artwork, programming, and meetings that consistently focus on reinforcing its guiding principles. Students notice this and they respect it.

Ultimately, your recruiting information should explain the growth opportunities and career ladders available to young employees. For Gen Y, it should talk about training and mentoring programs. For Gen Z, it should also talk about opportunities for individual growth and development. In addition, your recruiting materials should emphasize how your people, as both individuals and professionals, live your corporate values.

Young people are looking for a work environment where the employees share their personal and professional ideals. The more you can connect them with people who are like them (alumni, affinity group members, other young employees), the more they will identify with you as an employer of choice.

Your Online Presence

Gen Y and Gen Z are highly educated, and they have access to more information than any previous generation. As such, you should expect them to know about your company and your roles prior to the interviews. While Gen Y may take your corporate information at face value, Gen Z is more likely to want proof that the stories are real. Both generations will respond well to videos on your company recruiting website or social media page of new hires talking about their experiences working for your company.

However, Gen Z is more likely to take the additional step of checking Glassdoor.com or Vault.com to see if they can find conflicting information. Gen Z grew up in the age of astroturfing (fake online reviews to improve product sales), so they tend to be warier of corporate information they see online.

Your online site should show how your company is changing the world. For example:

1. If you are a bank, how did your work help grow a business and create jobs?
2. If you are a manufacturer, how did you provide more value or quality for your customers? Or, did your firm apply manufacturing principles to help a local non-profit?
3. If you are an engineering firm, how did your work help create roads that allow rural communities greater access to jobs and resources?

And it should also show how your employees are changing the world:

1. Did your employees adopt a local non-profit or cause?
2. Do you have pictures of your employees volunteering at a food bank?
3. Do you allow paid time off for volunteer activities?
4. Do you have employees with notable accomplishments or hobbies?
5. Do you have video interviews with new hires talking about why their work matters?
6. Do you profile employees with interesting jobs or hobbies?

Make sure other sites match the message you're sending. Are you listed as a sponsor or supporter on the non-profit sites you feature? Does the online news about you present you as a good corporate citizen? Are your employees saying positive things about you and each other on social media and online review sites? If you have not already implemented social media policies to ensure this is happening, see Chapter 4, "Productivity."

In addition, your online site should include clear information about job opportunities, career paths, recruiting processes, and timelines. Videos of recent hires or interns talking about their work are great, but make sure the videos reflect the culture and diversity of your organization.

Be careful with your profiles and videos, though. I had a company that asked their summer interns to make a video talking about their internship experiences so the company could use it in their recruiting efforts. This was a great idea, but the video wound up demonstrating the complete lack of diversity in their internship program, which resulted in an even less diverse applicant pool the following year.

Interview Processes

As I mentioned earlier, I've noticed a trend in employers moving to virtual career fairs and web-based interviews. Their argument is that the current generation is more comfortable with virtual communication. While this is true, it is not how they want to select an employer. Virtual job fairs continue to be something students largely distrust, which results in employers more likely seeing only those students who are not in high demand.

Despite the preponderance of virtual communication, the younger generations still make their career decisions based on relationships. Thus, those companies who heavily emphasize videotaped interviews, virtual job fairs, and online assessment tests may actually be preventing the very top students from applying for their jobs—unless they have already developed a relationship with those students. The best and brightest candidates have many options available to them, and a cumbersome or impersonal process will not attract them.

The relationship-based, interpersonal interview process has stood the test of time. If you are already a "prestige employer" who has strong relationships with faculty and students, then you can sometimes put students through an initial assessment or even a video interview screen in your first round screening process. For most companies, though, it will result in losing some of the stronger applicants who are being actively courted by other companies.

Young employees want to get to know their future coworkers and managers as people as well as professionals. They intend to have friendships at work. This is part of what motivates them to work hard on the job, so it shouldn't be discouraged. Lunches or dinners with candidates and a selection of young employees and managers are great ways to not only get to know the candidate, but also to ensure both the company and the candidate feel good about the cultural fit.

Along those lines, internships are among the very best ways to select new hires. Many Fortune 100 companies have moved to a process of only making college hires from their internship pools. Internships allow you 6-10 weeks to get to know a young employee and see how he or she works in your organization—all while getting some extra work done. While the days of unpaid internships are largely behind us (due to so many lawsuits from interns over Fair Labor Standards Act violations), hiring interns as temporary employees is much less expensive than making a bad hiring decision from the shorter, traditional interview process.

Students also benefit from the internship process, since it allows them time to make sure they are committed to the company or industry they have selected. The younger generation is frequently berated for leaving employers after a short time, and internships can alleviate some of this. It is worth mentioning that Generation X was also berated for "job hopping" when they were first graduating from college. All of the generations after the Baby Boomers experienced unpredictable economies where layoffs were common, and defined benefit plans, such as pensions, were being eliminated. In other words, companies stopped creating cultures of long-term loyalty to employees, so new employees entered the workforce with a self-preservation mindset.

Another challenge for young employees is that they have limited experience, so they may not always make the best career choices. This often results in employees leaving jobs in a shorter timeframe, to the dismay of employers, in order to pursue different opportunities or return to school to retrain. Internships are among the best ways to overcome this challenge, so new employees join your organization committed to their careers and clear in their expectations.

According to a 2009 survey by the National Association of Colleges and Employers, almost 40% of employers reported a higher five-year retention rate among employees they'd hired via their internship programs compared to other hires.[40] Hence, internships aren't just an altruistic way to help young people learn new skills and demonstrate learning on the job; they're also a way to save money for your company through improved hiring and increased retention.

Generational Interview Questions

Ultimately, the types of interview questions you ask will depend on the knowledge, skills, and abilities required for the position you are filling. As a former recruiting manager, I still prefer behavioral interviews—where candidates are asked to give examples of times they have been in situations relevant to the position, and how they handled them. There are some specific questions I would recommend to help you assess any generational issues that may arise.

---

40 "2009 Experiential Education Survey," *NACE Research Brief* (March 2009), accessed June 30, 2017, http://www.immagic.com/eLibrary/ARCHIVES/GENERAL/NACE_US/N090318E.pdf.

1. Tell me about a time you had to solve a problem, but you didn't know what to do, and how you handled it.
   a. For Gen Y: Were they able to work independently when appropriate to solve problems on their own?
   b. For Gen Z: Did they reach out for help when appropriate to solve problems within the existing structure?
2. Tell me about a time you made a mistake that impacted others, and how you handled it.
   a. For Gen Y: Did they take responsibility and handle it directly, or did they need to involve a manager to solve the problem?
   b. For Gen Z: Did they accept responsibility and let their manager know about the situation, or did they solve it without notifying anyone of the problem?
3. If you were hired, what would be your five-year plan after being hired?
   a. For Gen Y: Do they have a realistic idea of the promotion timeline and what is required to achieve it?
   b. For Gen Z: Do they plan to stay with your company for more than a year or two?
4. Tell me about a time you had a co-worker or group member challenge you and how you handled it.
   a. For both generations: Can they effectively and assertively handle difficult conversations?
5. Tell me about a time you had to manage multiple priorities with competing deadlines and how you handled it.
   a. For both generations: What time management and prioritization skills have they already developed?

Onboarding Young Employees

Once your new employee is hired, if you want to get the best from him or her, it is important that you have a plan to keep them engaged, coached, and nurtured. Basically, this is when the "care and feeding" part begins.

First and foremost, you should immediately create an environment where your young employees can all get to know one another and begin to bond. "Welcome Aboard" happy hours, pot-luck welcome lunches, or even welcome signs that are autographed by the entire office are a good, inexpensive start. For larger companies with more new hires, welcome receptions and parties are a great way to make your young employees feel at home, and to help them start connecting with their new coworkers. In my own department, I make a habit of inviting new employees to make coffee runs with me, just so we can visit informally.

Mentoring

The best companies have mentor programs where young employees are formally paired with mid-level employees who can coach them through realistic expectations, corporate politics, and best practices. It is important that the mid-level employees doing the mentoring are also recognized and rewarded for their work, because a good mentor can make a big difference in the long-term success of a young employee. A good mentorship program includes a component where the new employee sets career goals and works with the mentor on tips and coaching to work toward those goals.

At the same time, you'll want to coach the mentors before they take on their mentoring roles. It is often worthwhile to bring in an external expert to assist with this training for larger programs. Your mentors will need tips on how to give effective feedback, and you'll need to set expectations for the types of learning that may be useful for young employees. For instance, many young employees struggle with when to raise an issue and when to walk away. Coaching mentors on how and when to encourage young employees to be assertive versus how and when to encourage them to let something go can be extremely useful to both the mentors and their mentees.

Training

Training seems to work best when it's hands-on and interactive, or at least video-based. Training manuals are seldom read. Training should also be done in small, topical, bite-sized chunks that can be taken and reviewed easily on demand. Use the examples of some of the top massive open online courses (MOOCs) for best practices in training.

The more your training can clearly explain expectations for performance, communication, productivity, authority, and advancement, the better. It's not enough to just have the old-fashioned sexual harassment videos and consider your training done—especially since these generations are already so much more aware of and trained on diversity issues than previous generations! You must also take *all* of your behavioral expectations and norms and make them explicit in your onboarding training. This is the best way to make sure young employees perform to your expectations.

Lastly, be clear with your new employee about the type of training and professional development she can expect going forward, as well as what resources are available to her for independent learning. For Gen Y, let her know who she should go to with different types of questions and when she should go to them. For Gen Z, let him know who he should go to for various types of approvals and when he should go to them.

The more clearly you set expectations up front with your young employees, the more successful you will both be.

Best Practices in Recruiting

1. Personal relationships with candidates can mean more than prestige or money in their decision-making process.
2. Gen Y and Z are interested in having meaning and purpose in the world. Your online presence, your employees, your headquarters, and your news should all have consistent messages around your values and mission.
3. Use internships in your recruiting processes to improve screening, selection, and retention of full-time hires.
4. Quickly bring young employees into your organization through social events and mentoring programs to improve their engagement and loyalty.
5. Set clear expectations from the very beginning so your young employees can be successful.

CHAPTER 7

Young Employees Grow Up

Given all that we know about Gen Y and the things we're discovering about Gen Z, what does this mean for the future?

The future is in good hands.

Gen Y and Gen Z will be transformational leaders who use their advanced communication tools and deeply held values of inclusion and diversity to work collaboratively with others to improve the world they live in. They are extremely entrepreneurial, with heroes who prove you no longer need to spend years "paying your dues" to be a successful business leader.

Mark Zuckerberg was only 28 when Facebook went public, and Andrew Mason was the same age when he started Groupon. These are today's role models in business. In 2011, Gen Y launched almost 160,000 startups each month, and 29% of all entrepreneurs were 20 to 34 years old.[11] The big-

41 "The Millennial Generation Research Review," *US Chamber of Commerce Foundation*, November 12, 2012, accessed July 5, 2017, http://www.uschamberfoundation.org/millennial-generation-research-review.

gest obstacle to them doing even more is that most of them can't qualify for a business loan, although sites like Kickstarter and GoFundMe are making even this unnecessary. The lesson here is that if you allow them to bring this entrepreneurial spirit into your company, they will take you places you never dreamed of going, and your business will grow. But if you try to hold them back, they'll take their ideas and start their own businesses without you.

Gen Y is more focused on the future than previous generations were at their age. Possibly as a result of living through the "Great Recession," Gen Y is more likely to start saving for retirement earlier than previous generations. According to a survey conducted by Transamerica, the median age when Boomers started saving for retirement was 35, whereas Gen X started at 27, and Gen Y are starting at 22.[42]

While retirement plans still aren't the best way to recruit young people, it's useful to note that this generation is more financially aware than previous generations. As much as Gen Y was criticized in the media as a "boomerang" generation for moving back home after college (much like their predecessors, Gen X), it's not generally due to irresponsible spending. Being accustomed to a comfortable standard of living does influence the return home somewhat for Gen Y, but it's not the only reason.

---

42 C. Collinson, "The Retirement Readiness of Three Unique Generations: Baby Boomers, Generation X, and Millennials," *Transamerica Center for Retirement Studies* (April 2014), accessed July 5, 2017, https://www.transamericacenter.org/docs/default-source/resources/center-research/tcrs2014_sr_three_unique_generations.pdf.

To understand this better, let's look at how the median home cost in the US has changed as a percentage of the median income in the US for the different generations.

Year	Median Household Income in Real Dollars	Median Home Price	Home Price as a Percentage of Income
1970	$9,867	$23,400	237%
1980	$21,023	$64,600	307%
1990	$35,353	$122,900	348%
2000	$50,732	$169,000	333%
2010	$60,236	$221,800	368%
2014	$66,632	$282,800	424%

Sources: US Census 2010, US Census 2015.

As you can see, buying an "average" home has become increasingly expensive over the years. And this is an *average* price. But it's not just about people wanting large houses. More often than not, it's about choosing neighborhoods with low crime rates and good schools, which have become increasingly expensive.

Meanwhile, the rapid increase in college expenses have saddled most new graduates with significantly higher debt loads than previous generations.

Year	Annual, 4-year, In-State Tuition & Fees in 2016 Dollars
1976-77	$2,600
1986-87	$3,110
1996-97	$4,560
2006-07	$6,860
2016-17	$9,650

Source: College Board 2016

As a result, the current generations are saddled with some of the highest student loan debts in the history of our nation, and this problem is projected to get worse. The US culture, which was founded on independence, has traditionally expected children to move away from home. However, the economic reality of rising education and housing costs—combined with challenging job markets—has resulted in a new profile that looks more like many other places in the world, with many generations living together in the same home due to high housing costs.

Already the term "Sandwich Generation" has been used to define Boomers and Gen X, since they often have both aging parents *and* adult children living in the home with them. At the same time that Gen Y is entering financial distress, the Matures and Baby Boomers are finding their retirement plans inadequate for their current financial realities. As a result, approximately 15% of adults are providing financial support both to a parent over 65 *and* at least one child.[43]

So why does this matter to you as a manager?

It's important to note that progressive and inclusive workplaces are designing programs and policies to allow for this new family reality. Debt counseling and financial planning services are among the new creative benefits offered by companies. The more secure an employee feels in their personal lives, the less likely they are to be looking for a new job or employer. Likewise, the less stress an employee is experiencing, the more productive he will be.

As a company, it is worthwhile to invest in benefit programs and training that help employees who are struggling with aging parents, student loan debts, and mortgage questions. And it doesn't have to be difficult. Partnerships with credit unions and financial planners are a good start. Flexible workplaces that provide or allow for both elder care and childcare are another. All of us at some point will be the aging family member in need of assistance, so it makes sense for our own futures to put programs in place now to help our employees with these issues.

---

43 K. Parker and E. Patten, "The Sandwich Generation: Rising Financial Burdens for Middle-Aged Americans," *Pew Research Center Social & Demographic Trends,* January 30, 2013, accessed July 5, 2017, http://www.pewsocialtrends.org/2013/01/30/the-sandwich-generation/.

Yes, each of the generations grew up in a different time, which has resulted in slightly different behaviors and expectations in the workplace, but in some ways we are all the same.

	Gen Y	Gen Z	All Generations
Expectations	Provide clear and specific instructions	Set clear limits with goals	Assume a misunderstanding before assuming incompetence
Communication	Leverage group and visual presentation skills	Leverage virtual and video communication skills	Be open to diverse communication styles
Productivity	Give praise with constructive feedback often	Give them opportunities to give feedback	Give specific praise at twice the rate of constructive criticism
Motivation	Focus on outcomes and meaning more than appearances	Embrace multitasking and focus on higher purpose more than tradition	Have achievably high goals with flexibility on processes and a focus on vision and mission
Recruiting	Focus on people, vision, and values	Focus on future possibilities and purpose	Use recruiting processes that reflect your corporate mission, vision, and values, as well as required competencies, while being inclusive

Teach your more seasoned employees to seek to understand the motivations and behaviors of the current generation before assuming these young employees cannot do their jobs well. Most are very bright and competent when they are trained properly. While young people communicate differently from older generations, they often bring new gifts into the workplace, like more visual communication tools, and they can be trained if you need their written or verbal communication styles to change.

As I've mentioned throughout the book, young employees are not only open to feedback, but they can also bring fresh ideas to your organization if you are willing to listen. As with all generations, young people will respond best to constructive criticism when it is specific and mixed with specific praise—ideally given at least twice as often as criticism. Notice when they are doing things well, and give them praise for good work. Then they will be much more open and eager to hear constructive criticism when it is needed. Don't lower standards for younger employees, but do allow flexibility on how they should achieve those goals. Their work styles may look different from those of older employees, but they are very productive since they are accustomed to living in high-stress, multitasking environments.

Lastly, be clear on your organization's purpose and values, and make sure your actions and recruiting messages align with who you say you are. The younger generations want to have meaningful work with an impact on the world around them and the future, so they won't tolerate a company that isn't honest about who it is.

I have had phenomenal employees who were regularly targeted by headhunters offering much higher pay at other companies, but they've rarely ever left just for more money. Every one of them valued the flexibility, purpose, recognition, and support they received in our organization more than they valued a higher paycheck. The ultimate lesson is this: Don't underestimate the value of treating your employees like people first and employees second.

In the end, people want to be valued and treated with respect, regardless of their generation. While generational trends are a great way to reframe perplexing behavior in older or younger employees, the best approach is always to keep communication open and embrace the value and differences that each individual brings to the workplace.

BIBLIOGRAPHY

"2009 Experiential Education Survey." *NACE Research Brief* (March 2009). Accessed June 30, 2017. http://www.immagic.com/eLibrary/ARCHIVES/GENERAL/NACE_US/N090318E.pdf.

Abel, Jaison, Richard Deitz, and Yaqin Su. "Are Recent College Graduates Finding Good Jobs?" *Federal Reserve Bank of New York Current Issues in Economics and Finance* 20, no. 1 (2014). https://www.newyorkfed.org/medialibrary/media/research/current_issues/ci20-1.pdf.

Akinbami, L.J., X. Liu, P.N. Pastor, and C.A. Reuben. "Attention Deficit Hyperactivity Disorder Among Children Aged 5-17 Years in the United States." *NCHS Data Brief* 70 (August 2011). Accessed July 2017. https://www.cdc.gov/nchs/products/databriefs/db70.htm.

Anderson, M. "How Having Smartphones (or not) Shapes the Way Teens Communicate." *Pew Research Center Fact Tank.* August 20, 2015. Accessed October 1, 2016. http://www.pewresearch.org/fact-tank/2015/08/20/how-having-smartphones-or-not-shapes-the-way-teens-communicate.

Ariga, Atsunori and Alejandro Lleras. "Brief and Rare Mental 'Breaks' Keep You Focused: Deactivation and Reactivation of Task Goals Preempt Vigilance Decrements." *Cognition* 118, no. 3 (March 2011), doi: 10.1016/j.cognition.2010.12.007.

Belinne, Jamie. *2011, 2016, 2017 GENB Student Surveys, Survey Results*. Houston: University of Houston, 2017.

Belinne, Jamie. *2010-2017 GENB Student Surveys, Survey Results*. Houston: University of Houston, 2017.

"The Big Payoff: Educational Attainment and Synthetic Estimates of Work-Life Earnings." *US Census* P23-210 (July 2002). Accessed July 5, 2017. https://www.census.gov/prod/2002pubs/p23-210.pdf.

Boland, Julie and Robin Queen. "If You're House Is Still Available, Send Me an Email: Personality Influences Reactions to Written Errors in Email Messages." *PLOS ONE* (March 9, 2016). Accessed July 5, 2017. http://journals.plos.org/plosone/article?id=10.1371/journal.pone.0149885.

Bryson, Ken and Lynne M. Casper. "Household and Family Characteristics: March 1997." *Census Bureau* P20-509 (April 1998). Accessed July 5, 2017. https://www.census.gov/prod/3/98pubs/p20-509.pdf.

Chandra, Anjani, Casey E. Copen, and Elizabeth Hervey Stephen. "Infertility and Impaired Fecundity in the United States, 1982-2010: Data From the National Survey of Family Growth." *National Health Statistcs Reports* 67 (August 14, 2013). Accessed July 5, 2017. https://www.cdc.gov/nchs/data/nhsr/nhsr067.pdf.

"Civil Cases." *Bureau of Justice Statistics Office of Justice Programs.* Accessed July 5, 2017. http://www.bjs.gov/index. cfm?ty=tp&tid=45.

Coley, Richard J., Madeline J. Goodman, and Anita M. Sands. "America's Skills Challenge: Millennials and the Future." *Educational Testing Service.* February 17, 2015. Accessed July 5, 2017. https://www.ets.org/s/ research/29836/.

Collinson, Catherine. "The Retirement Readiness of Three Unique Generations: Baby Boomers, Generation X, and Millennials." *Transamerica Center for Retirement Studies* (April 2014). Accessed July 5, 2017. https://www.transamericacenter.org/docs/de-fault-source/resources/center-research/tcrs2014_sr_three_ unique_generations.pdf.

Conner, Cheryl. "Who Wastes the Most Time at Work?" *Forbes.* September 7, 2013. Accessed July 5, 2017. http://www. forbes.com/sites/cherylsnappconner/2013/09/07/ who-wastes-the-most-time-at-work.

Cooper, Sir Cary. "It Pays to Play." *BrightHR.* October 29, 2015. Accessed July 5, 2017. https://pages.brighthr. com/itpaystoplay-v3.html.

Dua, Tanya. "Inside Taco Bell's Snapchat Strategy." *Digiday.* August 13, 2015. Accessed July 5, 2017. http://digiday. com/brands/inside-taco-bells-snapchat-strategy/.

Emojipedia. "Snapchat Emoji Meanings—Friend Emojis." Accessed July 2017. http://emojipedia.org/snapchat/.

Epstein, Eli. "Why Taco Bell Went Loco for Snapchat and Millennials." *Mashable.* May 29, 2014. Accessed July 5, 2017. http://mashable.com/2014/05/29/taco-bell-marketing-strategy/#RGGLD1s9uiqj.

Fry, R. "This Year Millennials Will Overtake Baby Boomers." *Pew Research Center Fact Tank.* January 16, 2015. Accessed September 2015. http://www.pewresearch.org/fact-tank/2015/01/16/this-year-millennials-will-overtake-baby-boomers/.

Gouveia, Aaron. "2013 Wasting Time at Work Survey." *Salary.com.* March 19, 2014. Accessed July 5, 2017. http://www.salary.com/2013-wasting-time-at-work-survey/.

Hiltzik, Michael. "Kodak's Long Fade to Black." *Los Angeles Times.* December 4, 2011. Accessed July 5, 2017. http://articles.latimes.com/2011/dec/04/business/la-fi-hiltzik-20111204.

"Historical Income Tables: Families." *US Census.* December 31, 2015. Accessed July 6, 2017. https://www.census.gov/data/tables/time-series/demo/income-poverty/historical-income-families.html.

"Labor Force Projections to 2020: A More Slowly Growing Workforce." *Bureau of Labor Statistics Employment*

Outlook: 2010-2020. February 21, 2012. Accessed July 17, 2017. https://www.bls.gov/opub/mlr/2012/01/art3full.pdf.

Lane, Sylvan. "Beyond Millennials: How to Reach Generation Z." *Mashable.* August 20, 2014. Accessed October 1, 2016. http://mashable.com/2014/08/20/generation-z-marketing.

Lee, Melissa. "Report Discloses SATs, Admit Rate." *The Harvard Crimson.* May 7, 1993. Accessed July 5, 2017. http://www.thecrimson.com/article/1993/5/7/report-discloses-sats-admit-rate-pa/.

Livingston, G. "Fewer Than Half of US Kids Today Live in a Traditional Family." *Pew Research Center Fact Tank.* December 22, 2014. Accessed October 1, 2016. http://www.pewresearch.org/fact-tank/2014/12/22/less-than-half-of-u-s-kids-today-live-in-a-traditional-family/.

Mander, Jason. "Facebook Slips as Instagram Rises." *GlobalWebIndex.* February 9, 2015. Accessed July 5, 2017. http://www.globalwebindex.net/blog/facebook-slips-as-instagram-rises.

Mathews, T.J. and B. Hamilton. "First Births to Older Women Continue to Rise." *NCHS Data Brief* 152 (May 1, 2014). Accessed July 5, 2017. https://www.cdc.gov/nchs/products/databriefs/db152.htm.

McSpadden, Kevin. "You Now Have a Shorter Attention Span Than a Goldfish." *Time.* May 14, 2015. Accessed July 5, 2017. http://time.com/3858309/attention-spans-goldfish/.

"Median and Average Sales Prices of New Homes Sold in United States." *US Census.* December 31, 2010. Accessed July 6, 2017. https://www.census.gov/const/uspriceann.pdf.

Melina, R. "Teen Smoking, Drinking Hits Lowest Levels Since 1970s." *Live Science.* December 15, 2011. Accessed October 1, 2016. http://www.livescience.com/17497-teen-cigarette-alcohol.html.

"The Millennial Generation Research Review." *US Chamber of Commerce Foundation.* November 12, 2012. Accessed July 5, 2017. http://www.uschamberfoundation.org/millennial-generation-research-review.

Molnar, A., G. Miron, L. Huerta, L. Cuban, B. Horvitz, C. Gulosino, J.K. Rice, and S.R. Shafer. "Virtual Schools in the U.S. 2013: Politics, Performance, Policy, and Research Evidence." *National Education Policy Center* (May 2, 2013). Accessed July 5, 2017. http://nepc.colorado.edu/publication/virtual-schools-annual-2013.

Parker, Kim and Eileen Patten. "The Sandwich Generation: Rising Financial Burdens for Middle-Aged Americans." *Pew Research Center Social & Demographic Trends.* January 30, 2013. Accessed

July 5, 2017. http://www.pewsocialtrends.org/2013/01/30/the-sandwich-generation.

Ray, B. "Research Facts on Homeschooling." *National Home Education Research Institute*. March 23, 2016. Accessed October 10, 2016. http://www.nheri.org/research/research-facts-on-homeschooling.html.

Schawbel, D. "10 New Findings About the Millennial Consumer." *Forbes*. January 20, 2015. Accessed October 2016. http://www.forbes.com/sites/danschawbel/2015/01/20/10-new-findings-about-the-millennial-consumer/.

"The High School Careers Study." *Millennial Branding*. February 3, 2014. Accessed October 1, 2016. http://millennialbranding.com/2014/high-school-careers-study/.

Sloane, Garett. "Snapchat's 'Crazy Engaged' Users Can't Resist a Message From Taco Bell." *AdWeek*. August 22, 2014. Accessed July 5, 2017. http://www.adweek.com/news/technology/snapchats-crazy-engaged-users-cant-resist-message-taco-bell-159677.

Snyder, Thomas D., Cristobal de Brey, and Sally A. Dillow. "Digest of Education Statistics 2015, 51st Edition." *Institute of Education Sciences National Center for Education Statistics* (December 2016). Accessed July 5, 2017. https://nces.ed.gov/pubs2016/2016014.pdf.

Sparks & Honey. "Meet Generation Z: Forget Everything You Learned About Millennials." *Slideshare.* June 17, 2014. Accessed July 5, 2017. http://www.slideshare.net/sparksandhoney/generation-z-final-june-17.

"Teen Drinking and Driving." *CDC Vital Signs.* Last modified October 2, 2012. Accessed July 5, 2017. http://www.cdc.gov/vitalsigns/teendrinkinganddriving/.

Thompson, Daphne. "Harvard Acceptance Rate Will Continue to Drop, Experts Say." *The Harvard Crimson.* April 16, 2015. Accessed July 5, 2017. http://www.thecrimson.com/article/2015/4/16/admissions-downward-trend-experts/.

"Tuition and Fees and Room and Board over Time, 1976-77 to 2016-17, Selected Years" *College Board.* December 31, 2016. Accessed July 5, 2017. https://trends.collegeboard.org/college-pricing/figures-tables/tuition-and-fees-and-room-and-board-over-time-1976-77_2016-17-selected-years.

Ventura, Stephanie, Brady Hamilton, and T.J. Mathews. "National and State Patterns of Teen Births in the United States 1940-2013." *National Vital Statistics Reports* 63, no. 4 (August 20, 2014). Accessed July 5, 2017. https://www.cdc.gov/nchs/data/nvsr/nvsr63/nvsr63_04.pdf.

Visser, Susanna N., Melissa L. Danielson, Rebecca H. Bitsko, Joseph R. Holbrook, Michael D. Kogan, Reem M.

Ghandour, Ruth Perou, and Stephen J. Blumberg. "Trends in the Parent-Report of Health Care Provider-Diagnosed and Medicated Attention-Deficit/Hyperactivity Disorder: United States, 2003-2011." *Journal of the American Academy of Child & Adolescent Psychiatry* 53, no.1 (January 2014). Accessed July 5, 2017. https://www.cdc.gov/ncbddd/adhd/features/key-findings-adhd72013.html.

Weissmann, Jordan. "The Decline of the American Book Lover." *The Atlantic.* January 21, 2014. Accessed July 5, 2017. http://www.theatlantic.com/business/archive/2014/01/the-decline-of-the-american-book-lover/283222/.

About the Author

J amie Belinne has worked with hundreds of managers and thousands of young people on recruiting and management issues for nearly three decades. During this time, she's seen the impact and challenges of many generations in the workplace. She is currently the Assistant Dean for Career Services at the C.T. Bauer College of Business at the University of Houston and President of the international MBA Career Services and Employers Alliance. Prior to this, Jamie managed recruiting and staffing at The University of Texas at Austin, where she also built and led the McCombs School of Business's first dedicated MBA Career Services division.

Jamie is the 2012 winner of the National Association of Colleges and Employers (NACE) Professional Change Maker Award for her initiatives around experiential education, and the winner of the 2013 NACE Innovation Excellence Award for Diversity Programming. She has consulted with organizations around the country on intergenerational management issues and productivity improvement, and she is the author of two award-winning textbooks focused on helping young people succeed in the workplace.

An avid athlete, Jamie was a member of Team USA 2009 for the ITU Long Distance Triathlon World Championships and Team USA 2011 for ITU Duathlon World Championships. She is also an IRONMAN, an RRCA-certified run coach, and a mother of a Gen Y son and a Gen Z daughter.

Made in the USA
Lexington, KY
02 October 2018